CW00348609

Asda Magic

by

David Smith

Grosvenor House
Publishing Limited

David Smith is hereby identified as author of this
work in accordance with Section 77 of the Copyright, Designs
and Patents Act 1988

The book cover picture is copyright to David Smith

This book is published by
Grosvenor House Publishing Ltd
28-30 High Street, Guildford, Surrey, GU1 3EL.
www.grosvenorhousepublishing.co.uk

A CIP record for this book
is available from the British Library

ISBN 978-1-908596-55-0

Contents

Foreword

"David and I joined Asda in 1994, within 30 days of each other, at a defining time. Fresh from our respective MBAs we pitched up in our respective departments (David in people, me in marketing), bristling with new ideas.

And what a stage to bring those ideas to life.

Asda at that time was a turnaround business, with no guarantee of future success. They were exciting and raw times, and we both had the privilege of playing key roles as the business introduced massive organisational change.

There's no doubt that the sense of urgency we both feel today has its genesis during those early Asda years.

David's book chronicles the history of Asda, with particular emphasis on the key elements to cultural change; engaging people; and, as a consequence, improving business performance.

And those principles are not just valid in turnaround businesses.

My period as chief executive of Asda focused on creating a business to deliver world class performance, in a hugely competitive sector, at a time of serious economic upheaval.

The cultural progress we made in the 1990's still underpins Asda's performance today, in different circumstances. I firmly believe high performance results from strong leadership; where people understand very clearly what's required of them, and they are engaged in the mission of their business.

Energising and engaging 170,000 people in a food retail business is an enormous task, but there is a vibrancy in Asda's people, which comes from the culture David helped to create.

I enjoyed reading this book, and I'm sure you will too. But 'enjoy' underplays the power of the Asda story David tells, and the rich seam of learning which he brings out, for those seeking to engage their people and obtain a higher business performance."

Andy Bond, chief executive of Asda 2005-2010

This book is dedicated to all my colleagues in Asda, from the shop floor in stores; from distribution centres & from Asda house & George house. I have known many of them personally over many years. Most of my best ideas and solutions to the problems of day to day management came from listening to those colleagues. I have been humbled by the dedication of so many people, to a business they so evidently cared about. I often said of many of those people that if you cut them open, they would 'bleed green'. This book attempts to do justice to those people... I salute them!

CHAPTER 1

Preamble
The musings of a people practitioner

"Practical men, who believe themselves to be quite exempt from any intellectual influences, are usually the slaves of some defunct economist. Madmen in authority, who hear voices in the air, are distilling their frenzy from some academic scribbler of a few years back."

Baron John Maynard Keynes 1883-1946
British Economist

This is a practitioners' book, not an academic research project. Many people put forward theories, but have no practical outworking of those theories. My preference is to talk about the ideas which I know have worked in practice.

Nevertheless, I am an avid reader of academics, gurus, and over the many years of my business career have read most of the research on the subject of 'human resources'. Don't you just hate those words! To me, people are people. Yes they are obviously a resource. Anyone who has studied economics knows that there are 3 basic resources, (capital, machinery or technology and people). But for me, and I would say this wouldn't I, it is people who matter most in any enterprise of whatever size or scale. Without people, nothing gets done and nothing is achieved. Businesses can have loads of capital, and indeed many are exceedingly cash rich, but without the right people, they will not perform to their highest potential. Some businesses are very capital constrained, yet have achieved amazing results. Moreover, in this age of fast copying, everything is replicable, with the only exception being your people.

I have spent all my corporate career… some 35 plus years in the area of people management, so yes I do have a view of what works well and what does not in terms of leading and managing. 19 of those years were spent in the UK coal industry, male dominated (by law only men could work underground), mostly full time workers, heavily capitalised, state owned in those days, heavily unionised (a closed shop originally) and the scene of the battle between the Thatcher government and trade union power in the 1980's. I learned a lot about people and behaviour, the balance of power and the media, through that experience.

I then began 15 years in the Asda supermarket business. A very different environment, but very much a people centric business. Asda employed over 170,000 people. Mostly female workers, mostly part-time, not particularly heavily mechanised and no longer heavily unionised. Asda was a fascinating case study of cultural change, from the turnaround of the 1990's, to the challenges of present day. Few businesses are 'blessed' with the opportunity of near bankruptcy, and the momentum that brings, in terms of a force for change. A business in trouble has the gift of everyone realising change needs to happen. It becomes a 'burning platform' for change.

This book is about the cultural journey at Asda over approximately 15 years through to 2008. This is a story I have been intimately involved with, and one which I hope will be useful to those wanting to drive a positive and thriving profitable culture in their own business. Culture drives engagement, which produces high performance when you get it right.

I joined Asda, after my Henley MBA, and was fascinated by the actions of Archie Norman and the team he was building at the time. Asda had gone from a business with £1 billion surplus to a £1 billion debt, due to the ill conceived acquisition of 60 Gateway stores and the furniture business MFI. This all took place in the late 1980's when interest rates on loans went through the ceiling. The Asda business was 10 days away from defaulting on its covenants, and would have been unable to pay its people, had it not been for two city financed rights issues of shares and a new turnaround plan.

I claim no input to that early strategic thinking. Much of that was in place when I arrived. What I do lay claim to, was being a part of the new operational team who made the strategy of the 'Asda way of working' come alive. It was hard work and a lengthy struggle, but absolutely fascinating at every juncture. One of the keys to making cultural change successful, is to stick at it. I'm not sure 'stickability' is a leadership term used by academics, but stickability is one principle I have based my management life upon. Stickability counts. A top performing leadership team has to be able to keep at it, even when everything looks pretty bleak.

CULTURAL CHANGE IS NO QUICK FIX

The road of cultural change is long. Victories are hard fought and take time. I can promise the reader no quick fixes. In my experience, life is not like that. You have to decide what is important, find out the things that work, and then grind out the change. You can build momentum, but cultural change will commence slowly. Jim Collins, in his book 'good to great', likens this to a flywheel effect, where rotation begins slowly but momentum builds over time.

People tend to get bored easily. All chief executives want quick results. In retail people get bored with initiatives in 'nanoseconds'. Retail seems to attract those leaders who enjoy things that move fast. In 'Belbin speak' they are fabulous shapers and originators, great starters but terrible completer-finishers. This phenomenon has necessitated constant refreshing/reinventing and reformatting of cultural change materials... without losing the principles of the culture. In my experience, you need to retain core principles and building blocks, but constantly refresh materials and approaches. Change needs to retain the core essence, but feel 'fresh' in order to maintain the interest and focus of those in the business in each successive business cycle.

For me, the principles I am about to discuss, are pretty timeless. As long as business continues to employ people, and I don't see that changing any time soon, then these strategic principles will continue to be the cornerstone of a strong and powerful culture... one which enables your business to be as profitable and successful as it can be (that of course assumes you have a workable, viable business model you want to drive... that's a pretty fundamental prerequisite).

A lot of what I am about to say cross correlates with much academic research and the work of some of the management gurus. As I said, I am an avid reader of the literature, but this is fundamentally a people practitioner's view of those things which work; things which are important; and things which hold true in the long term. High performance is about accessing discretionary effort, by engaging your people in the 'cause' of your business. It's about winning the heart and soul of your people.

THE IMPORTANCE OF A SOUND BUSINESS STRATEGY

Mission – purpose – and underpinning values

What I am not trying to say, is that if you do the things embedded in this book, then your business will automatically succeed.

You must first have a sound business model, clear strategy, be in touch with your customer and deliver the goods or services which meet their needs now, and into the future. If you do have a successful business idea, or a business model which you know can succeed in the marketplace, then these principles will act as enablers to make your business the best it can be. I do hate books which recommend action, but never acknowledge the wider business context!

Asda had a sound business model. Asda's mission was 'to be Britain's best Value retailer, meeting the needs of customers… always'. Best value meant price leader. Everyday low prices… which could be relied upon, and it is no surprise that Asda won the Grocer magazine basket survey of 33 commonly purchased items (which change slightly by the season for salads in summer / soups and staples in winter) including bread/milk etc for 13 years running. Yes, that was every single year consistently.

Asda had laser focus on price and value, because it had a purpose. That purpose, which galvanised people behind something worth fighting for, was 'to make goods and services more affordable for everyone'. Asda was about bringing down the cost of living for people, and that felt like a worthwhile cause to the people working in the business.

To be the lowest price operator, Asda had to operate at the lowest cost. Efficiency was really important in making a low margin business work… and this is where the cultural enablers assume such a high degree of importance.

Asda believed that by being a truly great place to work, it could become a great place for customers to shop. Miserable people cannot give legendary service. It is an oxymoron. You can put them through as many customer service programmes as you like, at great expense, but you are wasting both time and money.

However, if you can get your people into that sweet spot of motivated performance, they will give great service and create a unique selling proposition. In this situation, the business model will begin to fly, and commercial success/profitability will be enhanced.

Asda moved from an ailing fourth ranking retailer in the early 1990's when I joined, to the strong UK number two, a position achieved in 2004. It is no amazement to me that Sainsbury was for many years Number one, and was overtaken for that top spot by both Tesco and Asda. You can never rest on past laurels in a competitive retail market, or the competition will 'eat your lunch'.

Asda utilised the phrase from the book 'Only the paranoid survive' by Andrew Grove – becoming itself constantly paranoid. Asda became a very self critical business. Never satisfied with performance. Even when performance was pretty good or at market level. Asda wanted continuous outperformance of the market. Even then, Asda would look at what was left 'on the table'. This is a very healthy mindset for a strong business. Never to be complacent. Being paranoid about your competition getting ahead of you keeps you sharp. Self flagellation is better than someone else giving you a beating!

There are thousands of examples of good businesses, with strong business models, who went to sleep and expected it all to continue. Marks and Spencer, prior to the Stuart Rose turnaround, would be the most classic example, and I'm sure we could all quote our own favourites of that 'gone to sleep' phenomenon.

STRATEGY HAS TO BE UNDERPINNED BY A HIGH PERFORMANCE CULTURE

Asda aimed to achieve a second unique selling point, after being lowest price in the market (or best value), and that was... having the friendliest service. Asda wanted customers to feel the warmth and friendliness of Asda people, and retail sector perception data indicated that Asda succeeded in creating a long term sustainable point of difference. Having the 'warmest' and most friendly service in the competitor set. The belief was that being the best place to work would enable Asda to be the best place to shop from a service perspective. Customer commentary also revealed the view that Asda people really were different, and that 'service edge' was tangible. More of that later.

THE 7 PRINCIPLES OF BUILDING A HIGH PERFORMANCE CULTURE

The major content of this book describes what I consider to be the 7 principles which enable a business to build a culture of high performance. To me, the question on the lips of every quality chief executive should be: "how can I get the best from my people, in order to outperform the competition?"

Before describing those principles, I want to introduce the importance to the Asda case study of having a low cost business model. I also want to explain the link between measurement and motivation. Finally, I want to pose the question for the reader: "can you create a high performance culture?"

Chapter 2

The importance of a low cost operation but with real personality

> "If we would have anything of benefit, we must earn it, and earning it becomes shrewd, inventive, ingenious, active and enterprising."
>
> Henry Ward Beecher
>
> "We would rather have one man or woman working with us, than three merely working for us."
>
> J Dabney Day

Cost cutting alone is not the answer. Friendly service has to be in the mix to achieve real differentiation from competitors.

Asda isn't the largest grocery retailer, that label falls to Tesco, and consequently they gain the advantages of economies of scale in buying, from their size. In order for Asda to offer the best prices to customers in the UK consistently, there had to be other efficiencies within the operation of the business to compete with Tesco's size (twice the market share of Asda).

My phrase for this is simple: Asda had to 'run faster' than the competition in order to make the business model work.

Asda had to continually find new ways of shipping goods; filling shelves and serving customers to increase efficiency. The business also integrated sustainability initiatives into the operation. For instance, Asda reduced fuel usage (per case of goods) by 23%, and had initiatives to reduce that still further.

With respect to serving customers; self service checkouts were adopted by 20% of the UK customer base, and the UK has become the leading country in the world with the number of customers wanting to 'self serve'. I am still amazed by how popular this is. All estimates of how big this was predicted to become were exceeded. For those customers who love to self serve those few quick items, they have assisted business productivity.

Being a great place to work also carried through into efficiency. When Asda colleagues became truly engaged in the business, with morale scores running in the 90%+ area, then this had a positive impact on the bottom line. Colleagues became shareholders, and were bonused on profit delivery. There was an overall halo effect of the high performance culture which the business was seeking to foster.

Giving real focus to efficiency led to the Asda business becoming the lowest cost operator in the marketplace.

Being the lowest cost operator of the big four supermarkets, enabled Asda to continue to offer the best prices in the market to customers. Asda's formula was that everyday low costs enabled everyday low prices. If Asda was not the most efficient operator, then the business model would falter.

Winning as Lowest Cost Operator

Cost of doing business (% sales)

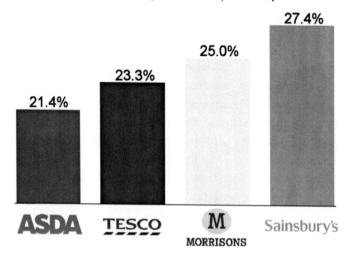

Diagram 1 – Winning as the Lowest Cost Operator

During the 1980s, Asda ran with margins which were too high and customers felt let down that they were not getting sufficient discount at Asda. The business lost its way as a consequence, and profits quickly declined as customers went elsewhere.

Asda has always been a value retailer at its core, with a service personality making a point of differentiation to customers. Asda talked for many years about "ordinary people doing extraordinary things", and I personally believe that this made a massive difference within the Asda formula and business model. Asda people became fiercely proud of the business they

11

worked for, and their service became 'legendary' as a consequence.

Let me pick out a few examples for you of the type of thing I'm talking about. Here is a holidaymaker in Cornwall:-

"I work in retail management, and I know that good reports are often not mentioned, yet the bad ones are very quick to come, and often for minor things. This note is to say that I wanted to thank your people at the St Austell Asda store, and in particular a very helpful and pleasant lady there. My family and I were on holiday in the area for the first time, and would normally shop at Tesco, yet we happened to pop into Asda to pick up a tea towel (essential when camping). This lady was busy stocking shelves when we asked her for help. At this point, rather than the service I have come to expect from most retailers, she stopped what she was doing and took us on a 'trek' across the shopfloor to the product, then to the next. Although it did not take very long, she was extremely polite and helpful. We then became regular visitors to this store, buying all our food for the 2 weeks we were on holiday. Everyone at the checkouts bid us a good day in one form or another. So, well done to them all! Our local Asda is 10 miles away in Corby. I will try them in future, and if we get the same attitude to service, you will have a new family of customers."

I think you can see how 'legendary' service becomes 'habit changing' for customers, and massively adds to business. This is a high performance culture at work, changing customer habits. Customers have choices, and in an increasingly homogeneous world, service can be a spectacular point of difference.

Here's another example, this time in one of Asda's newer formats, an Asda Living store on the Crown Point retail park in Leeds. Again a customer letter tells the story:- "I wanted to let you know about a brilliant shopping experience I had in your store at Crown Point yesterday evening around 5.30pm. I had come in to purchase a stair gate to keep my young daughter at bay! Whilst I was there, I couldn't see a price on a display for pram umbrellas. I found a young girl replenishing nappies close by. She obviously saw me approaching out of the corner of her eye, and turned around before I had even reached her, with a big smile and asked if I was alright and whether she could help me with anything? She went to the till to find the price of the umbrella, and whilst I was waiting, I picked up the stair gate and a few other bits. As she came back, she was really smiley, and offered to take the gate and my other bigger items to leave at the till for me, whilst I carried on shopping. It was such a pleasure to be greeted by such a fab person and to be offered help. It really does make a refreshing change to speak to someone who cares about what you need, and doesn't just say 'I don't know', or 'go and ask at the till'. She really was fantastic, and I wanted to let you know that it is the first time in a long time that I have left anywhere so impressed with the service, and have spoken to someone who couldn't have done more for you."

It is a fact that customers tell more people about bad service than good. It does change their behaviour, and in some cases they may no longer shop with you. However, good experiences also 'carry' to other customers, and change shopping habits positively.

Lest you think these are isolated examples, let me give you some more. Here's a story about an Asda store in Devon in Newton Abbott:- "I went to your store in Newton Abbott, and asked someone filling shelves where the marshmallows were which I couldn't find. He immediately stopped what he was doing and offered to take me. I said that he just needed to tell me where they were, and I would find them. He insisted on taking me, and said it would be his pleasure to do so. I asked him who his boss was, and he said that I was the boss... the customer. I subsequently found the store manager to complement him on the service in store. The store manager told me he had joined Asda from another retailer, and he absolutely loved Asda. He had waited for four years to see whether the Asda 'bubble' would burst, but he eventually realised it wasn't going to, and that Asda truly was a great place to work. This is deeply impressive."

Some of the legendary service stories extend beyond the actual service itself into human relationships. The next story I am about to tell, illustrates that situation very well:- "I would like to make you aware of a wonderful person you have working at your Asda Tipton store. Just recently, I was unfortunate enough to be diagnosed with 'advanced breast cancer, and my prognosis was that I required a double mastectomy, with subsequent treatments after the operation. I was obviously extremely distressed at the news, and finding it very difficult to accept. My operation was scheduled for July, and as I expected some sunshine, I went to my local Asda with a view to purchasing a sun lounger so I could help my recovery from surgery in the garden. As I was looking at the sun loungers, an Asda assistant came and asked if I needed any help. I explained that I would like to see the sun lounger, and she very willingly obliged. During this time, we engaged in conversation, and due to my very low state, I told her the reason for the purchase of the sun lounger. To my amazement, she told me that she herself had also had a double mastectomy several years earlier, and proceeded to speak to me in a very positive and inspirational manner. She excused herself and returned with a piece of paper, on which she had written her telephone number. She then very kindly told me I was free to contact her at any time for advice, or just to discuss my fears and concerns. Several days later, I telephoned her, and we talked for two hours on the telephone. I found her witty and charming, very supportive, and truly inspirational. Just last week, I had my mastectomy, and was delighted to have a huge bouquet of flowers delivered to the hospital ward from this lady, with a very positive message in a beautiful card. I am hoping that Asda has some sort of reward for outstanding customer service. This lady has far exceeded the duties of an Asda store assistant. She offered me, a complete stranger, hope and support, and I feel that you as a company should be made aware of here wonderful qualities."

We sent that colleague and her family for a break at Eurodisney to recognise what she had done for that distressed shopper, but that is not the point of my story. The point is that friendly service with personality reaches out to the customer, and touches them in unexpected ways. This is why Asda sought to become a high performance / low cost operation. There is a very compelling graph in Kotter and Hesketh's 'Corporate culture and performance' which shows the data of 207 companies in 22 different industries over a period of 11 years. The difference in growth results from companies with a performance enhancing culture is remarkable:-

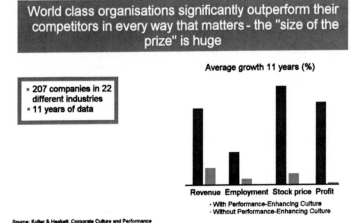

Diagram 2 – World class organisations

Asda had a low cost/strong culture formula which was built over many years. This was neither easy nor simple to execute, but it produced a winning formula.

To further illustrate the effect upon customers, I pulled out a few blogs from the internet:-

The first are from the online discussion forum of Heat magazine:

"Asda for me. I always think their staff are nicer and more approachable than most supermarkets."

"I work at Sainsbury's and I like some of their stuff and they have good offers, buuuuttt my loyalty lies with Asda coz I think they are GREAT! When I was pregnant with my second one, I went to Asda and bought everything I needed for my baby in one shop!! How cool is that?"

Here are some more blog comments on Asda service from a variety of internet sites:

"I went swimming last night with my daughter, and as we were walking home I suggested a trip to Asda for fruit (we're on a health kick). I had £14.10 in my pocket (didn't take purse) and my shopping came to £14.70. I just said no problem, put the milk back, but the nice cashier said no need – have it with a 'smiley face'. What they do is if you're a bit short at the till (under £1) they will let you have the shopping anyway and put a smiley face ticket in the till so it all tallys."

"I like Asda's approach to customer service – at Christmas I was overcharged for a couple of bottles of port – I was refunded instantly and given a £2.00 gift card."

"A while ago we went shopping at Asda, and when we got home we'd got two less bags than we'd bought. We went back in case we'd left them at the checkout by accident but hadn't (don't know what happened to them). The customer service lady told us to take off the shelf what we'd left for free! I couldn't believe it."

"Yes ASDA come tops in customer service."

There is a virtuous circle in low cost; low prices and legendary service. Getting these things right or wrong is something customers certainly notice. Everything a retail business does is immediately noticeable and tangible for customers. No mistake........friendly service is a big deal.

CHAPTER 3

High performance must be tangible - measurement and motivation

"The man who trusts men will make fewer mistakes, than he who distrusts them."

Camillo di Cavour

"He that is of the opinion money will do everything, may well be suspected of doing everything for money."

Benjamin Franklin

"The wonder is, not that the field of stars is so vast, but that man has measured it."

Anatole France

Looking back over the past 100 years there has been a wealth of thinking and comment on reaching the utopia of high performance. You can reference Henry Gantt and his Gantt chart circa 1900. F. W. Taylor was looking into the principles of scientific management on the assembly line of the model T Ford in 1910, and by the 1930s, Elton Mayo was experimenting with worker behaviour at the Hawthorne works of the Western Electric company.

The 1940s were the War years and saw the invention of assessment centres by the War office, and Raymond

Cattell's measurement of personality via the 16 P F Scale. Peter Drucker began his thesis on the corporation, and management by objectives.

The 1950s saw the work of Fredrick Herzberg and Abraham Maslow around the whole topic of motivation, which was refined and amplified by Douglas McGregor's theory X and theory Y, all of which urged management to become more participative. At this time, Edward Deming was also writing about total quality management techniques and Japanese production methods. Kurt Lewin was also writing about group dynamics. By the 1960s, Peter Drucker was emphasising the importance of innovation, and John Kotter was writing about organisational culture, change and strategic leadership.

In the 1970s Tom Peters began the whole quest for excellence, and Chris Argyris was writing about the learning organisation. James McGregor Burns was discussing the topic of transformational leadership linked to change. The 1980s heralded more work on strategic thinking by Michael Porter, so beloved by MBA programmes, particularly based on the 5 forces. Hamel and Prahalad were both propounding the need for organisations to define core competencies, whilst Richard Boyzatis was also discussing the competent manager and competency theory.

The 1990s heralded ground breaking work by Daniel Goleman around emotional intelligence and its application to business. Whilst Stephen Covey was writing about the seven habits of highly effective people. Jim Collins wrote about the importance of vision;

mission; values and big hairy audacious goals. Robert Kaplan captured a lot of management practice around use of a balanced scorecard. The 'noughties' since 2000, have been a little bare of new 'ground breaking' ideas from the guru's and theorists. Perhaps the only new idea of note is around lean thinking, and the lean enterprise, which is not really attributable to one individual alone.

You may have heard of some or all of these theorists and thinkers, (this was not intended as a comprehensive review) you may have heard of just a few. Why do I give you this tour of management thinking over the past century? Mainly because I want to illustrate the theoretical underpinning of my own thinking around what was done in the sphere of people, management and leadership in Asda.

In my own view, some of the guru's are involved in merely 'fad surfing'. I have never bought into the whole competency debate myself, and have seen it stultify appraisal processes, and set people on a quest to be good at things they will never be good at. I'm firmly in the camp that people are born with certain strengths and capabilities, and are formed as 'square pegs' or 'round pegs'. They should be put into the right holes accordingly. There is very little return for trying to fit square pegs into round holes. I'm with Marcus Buckingham on his thinking around playing to people's inherent strengths. That's where you make most traction, by harnessing what's there already, and making it stronger.

Let's go back to what I personally believe is most important in the last 100 years of management thinking. F. W. Taylor was the first theorist to look at organised work when he defined his scientific theory of management. He was looking at the first production line, that of the model T Ford. His thoughts were based on the fact that he believed workers did not like work. Consequently, because of this belief, people needed to be measured, watched and carefully controlled. This authoritarian approach shaped so much of modern business as we know it today, that it cannot be ignored. We still tend to believe that 'what gets measured gets managed' and this belief comes straight from Taylorist thinking. Many of the thoughts around basic management skills (planning; organising and controlling work) emanate from that early frame of reference. We now know that much of Taylor's beliefs about human nature were inadequate, but some of the basic disciplines of management were useful.

In the Asda business, everything was measured. I have often said that retail businesses tend to measure everything that moves. From time to time, store managers in the Asda chain would give a huge 'push back' to the centre, on the number of measures they were subject to, and a cull would take place as a result of that feedback. It never took very long before new measures then began to creep back. I regard this as part of the natural 'ebb and flow' of a healthy business, but measurement should never be ignored. Without measurement, you don't know how well or badly you are doing. Taylor was certainly right about that, and many of his management disciplines still hold good today.

The next interesting development for me was the work of Elton Mayo in the 1930s. I remember first learning about his work when I was at college in Sheffield in the 1970s. It was like a 'light going on moment' for me... as it was for him. Until the time of Mayo, most attempts to improve performance and increase output were based on the assumption that the major incentives for humans were greed and fear, and that the worker could be regarded as a machine, whose output could be increased by improving physical conditions, and by eliminating wasteful movements or things causing fatigue.

Mayo questioned all these assumptions as a result of the findings of studies carried out at the Hawthorne works of the Western Electric company. Previous investigations of low morale in this company had proved inconclusive. The results of one study of lighting conditions indicated that every change introduced, resulted in increased output. Moreover, as those of you who know this piece of work will know, a control group who had no changes to their lighting also saw increased output. Mayo concluded, after a variety of experiments, that the increase in output could not be attributed to any of the changes to physical conditions, but were due to change in the attitude of the workers. The very fact that research was being carried out meant that someone was taking an interest in them, and they were made to feel important and responsible, and they responded by giving of their best. The interest shown; the need for their co-operation; and the fact that they were consulted about changes had transformed individual workers into a group whose members valued their membership, and wanted to meet group standards. Mayo's work pointed to the importance of human and social factors in work, and meant that work could no longer just be seen as a technological process with measures and controls. It may seem elementary to us today to realise the importance of this, but it was not until the 1950s (another 20 years) before motivational thinking began to establish itself (via Maslow and Herzberg) and much longer before managers in businesses realised the need to change their 'modus operandi'.

I believe many people in business today still do not realise the power of participative management, and are working on outdated and outmoded beliefs about managing people.

I'm always fascinated when I talk to groups of people, that almost everyone going into a management role has heard of Maslow, but very few really understand the application of what he was saying. Bearing in mind this body of work is nearly 60 years old, it is poorly understood. Based upon discussions with thousands of managers over my career, everyone remembers the triangle and the hierarchy of needs. They all recollect the need for such basic necessities as food and water (which come at the base of Maslow's pyramid), and some even remember that 'self actualisation' comes at the top of the pyramid (but no one knows what self actualisation means!). This is a classic of learning by wrote, not by understanding!

Apologies to those of you who know your motivational theory well, but here is Maslow's hierarchy as a refresh:-

self-
actualization
morality, creativity,
spontaneity, acceptance,
experience purpose,
meaning and inner potential

self-esteem
confidence, achievement, respect of
others, the need to be a unique individual

love and belonging
friendship, family, intimacy, sense
of connection

safety and security
health, employment, property, family and social stability

physiological needs
breathing, food, water, shelter, clothing, sleep

Diagram 3 – Maslow's Heirarchy

Maslow actually argued that only when a lower need
had been satisfied does the next level become
dominant, and the attention of the individual will be
turned to satisfying that higher need. A starving person
will take considerable risks to feed themselves if they
are in that position, but once that need is satisfied,
then protection from danger will become important.
Maslow's view was that only unsatisfied needs could
motivate behaviour of any kind. People can be partially
satisfied in any of the levels, and some individuals can
jump up to higher level needs, or down if for instance
they experience sudden change. Man is a 'wanting'
individual, and all the needs can be satisfied to some
extent in the work situation, and the lesson for the

leader is to realise that all needs must be considered in an attempt to motivate people.

Herzberg built very much on Maslow's thinking, considering that mankind has two sets of needs – those which are about maintenance, and those which are about motivation. The maintenance needs, or hygiene factors, are about avoiding pain or dissatisfaction. Working conditions; pay and social relationships at work are all hygiene factors. Clearly, any leader or employer cannot ignore getting these things right at a basic entitlement level, but they will not motivate. They will merely lessen the level of dissatisfaction.

Herzberg argued that the motivators are around the need for growth; development; responsibility and recognition. These human needs can only be met through what is actually done, that is, the work itself. The job itself is a much more powerful motivator than had previously been thought. Herzberg argued that employees at all levels could only be satisfied when the actual work is perceived to be meaningful and challenging by the worker.

This thinking is 60 years old. Let me say that again. This thinking is 60 years old! Everyone thinks we know all this stuff! So why do so many companies ignore it in what they actually do? So much management practice has been around changing the work environment; pay & bonus structures; terms & conditions; job security and supervision – yet none of these things are motivators, they merely ameliorate dissatisfaction. We have seen, through the example of the global banking crisis just how dysfunctional the focus on huge bonuses can become.

Let me do just a little more 'teaching grannie to suck eggs' if I may. My favourite piece of theoretical insight around this whole area of measurement and motivation, is that of Douglas McGregor. For me, his definitions are perhaps the most helpful in crystallising the debate. I just have a slightly different conclusion. McGregor describes two approaches to management – theory X and theory Y. Theory X describes 'traditional' management assumptions. These are that man is inherently lazy and unambitious, prepared to work only when it is unavoidable, and loathe to seek responsibility (a very Taylorist view). Theory X would suggest that direction, motivation and control must come from outside – and employees have to be driven by greed; fear and coercion. McGregor argues that managing under theory X causes a defensive reaction from workers, who are resentful of the rules, and will try to beat the system wherever possible. In working against the system, the workforce reinforces management's belief that the workforce is inherently bad. It is a vicious circle. In this situation, where (in 'Maslow speak') higher level needs are not being satisfied, people will tend to try to meet frustrated higher level needs as best they can, with demands for higher pay and job security. This again merely reinforces the vicious circle of false management belief.

McGregor developed a second set of assumptions based on a 'modern' view, which he termed 'theory Y'. This theory suggests that work is a natural human activity which is capable of providing enjoyment, and that external controls (carrot and stick) are not the only means of getting people to do good work. McGregor argued that people can exercise self control and self direction. If they are committed to the objectives to which they are working, individual higher level needs can be satisfied in the pursuit of organisational goals. McGregor's view was that the main task of management and leadership, was to create the 'conditions' where work leads to satisfaction and a sense of achievement. To enlist people's commitment to organisational goals, and arouse a sense of responsibility in the individual that what they are doing has real meaning and significance. Understanding and mutual target setting at all levels is therefore hugely significant.

I really like McGregor's work, because although it is now 60 years old, it has stood the test of time. My own refinement, is that there are certain elements of Theory X, such as measurement of all aspects of performance, and the making of effective strategic choices, which have to be carried out by executives. But, the more time spent on listening to the troops and getting them engaged in the goals of the organisation, the more productive the enterprise will become. The terminology used in the 1950s may seem a little out of date today, since the language has moved on to talking about 'employee engagement', but the principles remain highly relevant.

We have recently seen the effect in the banking sector of high levels of financial bonus driving behaviour which is not conducive to organisation health. This has had a disastrous impact upon global stability, and economies around the world. We're still living in a 'Taylorist' time warp in so much of what happens in business. Why does that occur, when our knowledge should have rendered that obsolete? We know better, but as leaders, we act in very similar ways to our predecessors 100 years ago.

No doubt money will always remain important in the minds of people, but it will always be a dissatisfier. When did anyone ever tell you they were paid too much? My personal focus for some time has been attempting to 'move the dial' on engaging people in business, and engendering real belief in what the business is trying to do. Recognition is more important than remuneration, and belief/involvement more powerful than rules and fear.

These are old lessons, 'nothing new', and yet so many businesses I talk to are still bound up in hierarchy and traditional command / control cultures. Others say that they have 'bought into' a progressive forward thinking culture. The truth is, they are just going through some of the motions of holding attitude surveys or subjecting leaders to 360° feedback, but they are not tackling the fundamentals of how their businesses operate. Their belief frame is still very 'old school'.

I would ask the question. What are your fundamental beliefs about the people you manage in your organisation? Do people come to work to be 'Luddites' and stop the job? Or do most people come to work wanting to succeed? What is your view? How do you manage? Are you forward thinking, and do you have a good understanding of the levers to building a high performance culture? Are you really connected to your people? How do you know?

Much of this is not new thinking. The problem, as always, is in making things happen. The challenge is also to make things happen in the right way. Execution is always the acid test. Can you get things done in the right way?

I worked in the Asda business for over 15 years, on getting things done willingly and really well, with and through others. I think the Asda business stumbled at times, was clumsy often, but was always working with that fundamental belief that 'people really do make the difference' in the business. There is more than a passing nod here to Elton Mayo; Maslow & Herzberg and Douglas McGregor. The Asda business never talked about the theory or the theorist, but attempted to embrace the principles in getting stuff done. Execution is always the bottom line.

I believe that one of the reasons that organisations find it so hard to change is often the people at the top. Boards and directors are too 'comfortable' with the 'traditional' management beliefs. Many don't wish to change, or find little compelling reason to do so. Asda was gifted with a 'cliff edge' experience of near bankruptcy, which certainly focused the mind around the need for change. Asda also had a collection of leaders who were enlightened, and wanted to employ new thinking to drive change.

I think Asda also achieved a good balance between measurement and motivation. There was a firm 'feet on the floor' practical approach to all that was done, whilst blending with an aspirational desire to get a level of performance that was 'emotionally fuelled' by high levels of involvement and commitment. Much effort over a long and sustained period of time, went into taking the ideas of the shopfloor to the highest levels, and to connect large numbers of people to the 'mission' and 'vision' of the business. Asda was more than a profit making entity; it was a 'family of people' who were committed to bringing down the cost of living for UK shoppers. That is something which is the 'essence' of the origins of Asda, and remains for many people employed within Asda, something worth 'getting up for' in a morning. It is an aspirational goal in a highly commercial and competitive sector.

Chapter 4

Can you create a high performance culture?

"Great works are performed not by strength but by perseverance."

Samuel Johnson

"The element of the unexpected and the unforeseen is what gives some of its relish to life, and saves us from falling into the mechanical thraldom of the logicians."

Winston Churchill

"We are living in a period which all too readily scraps the old for the new... As a nation, we are in danger of forgetting that new is not true because it is novel, and that the old is not false because it is ancient."

Joseph Kennedy

"It must be remembered that there is nothing more difficult to plan, more doubtful of success, nor more dangerous to manage than the creation of a new system. For the initiator enmity of all who would profit by the preservation of the old institutions, and merely lukewarm defenders in those who would gain the new ones."

Niccolo Machiavelli

The answer to the question in the chapter title has to be yes. Or why am I writing a book which sets out 7 principles of building a high performance culture?

Nevertheless, the reason I pose this question is that there are a lot of cynics out there. You know who you are! You may well be reading this book with a healthy dose of 'cynicism', which says "I don't believe there is any magic in Asda, and this whole cultural thing is much over hyped." Clearly, you are entitled to your view. I have a contrary one, based on a lifetime of business practitioner experience, and some tangible results to back up my belief. I'm sure that a few of the UK's major banks were organisations which claimed a strong link between employee engagement and the commercial performance of their bank. I can think of at least a couple. When things have gone so badly wrong, where are those arguments today?

My contention would be that you have to be doing the 'right things' both ethically and strategically, as well as engaging people in a high performing culture. The fact that your people are highly motivated will not make you succeed if you are simply making a strategic error or simply doing the wrong things. Hopefully, in an 'open' organisation, some people will be giving warning signals which are both heard and responded to, where people feel things are heading in the wrong direction. (hopefully... unlike the banks you are not firing whistleblowers in order to quell any warning voices!)

When Asda started off down the road of turning around the business, the term 'engagement' was not in vogue.

The 'buzzword' of that time was 'empowerment'. I'm sure many will remember that era very well.

Whether you are a fan of the term, 'engagement' or 'empowerment', or neither, these terms are all pointing to the importance of a motivated workforce in achieving results. To me it is obvious that all businesses employ people, and their creativity; ingenuity and incremental additional effort must make a difference, if it is deployed in the right direction. There is a level of discretionary effort which is accessible if people become 'switched on'. In many cases, the organisation is managed is such a way that this effort never comes to the surface. Some organisations are high performing for a time, but not on a sustained basis. My contention would be that you have to have the patience to make cultural change over the long term. This is something which took place over years at Asda, not a 'flash in the pan'. High performing businesses have to be able to make change happen; they have to have a shared sense of purpose; and they have to be close to meeting the needs of customers.

Asda spent a long time tapping into the discretionary effort of colleagues within the business. I believe that the reward for managing and leading people well is that they will give additional effort over and above the norm, and the happiness of people will spill over into legendary customer service. The huge question being examined by many organisations and thinkers is inevitably "does this translate into tangible organisational high performance?"

In their book 'Hard facts, dangerous half truths and total nonsense', Jeffrey Pfeffer and Robert Sutton, from

Stamford University, argue that most managers have fairly set ideas about the way the world works. There needs to be evidence rather than 'prejudice and beliefs' to back up what is being said. I am a believer in producing facts to back up what you are saying. There is no reason why people initiatives should not be measured, and also have a financially tangible return on investment. This book will conclude with some results and financial measures to silence the healthy cynics!

The Chartered Institute of Personnel & Development has recognised the need to get inside the 'black box' of people performance. They commissioned professor John Purcell of the university of Bath to investigate what was actually happening in companies getting success from high performance working. Purcell examined the link between discretionary behaviour, employee attitudes and business performance. Purcell's findings include the fact that high performance organisations have a 'big idea'. They have a clear sense of mission delivered through values and culture. This was definitely my experience at Asda. The desire to bring down the cost of living for customers was a big idea from Asda's early days in the 1960s; was subsequently resurrected in Asda's renewal in the 1990s, and exists in the Asda of the 21st century.

Purcell also talks about the role of the line manager in high performance working. I absolutely agree that managers play a key role in bringing involvement, and thereby engagement, to life. They give people space to perform, they coach, they encourage and recognise performance. You will see me pick up on these themes in my seven principles of a high performance culture.

The Institute for Employment Studies also has a view on this area of engagement. Their research in 2004 suggested that autonomy/satisfaction, together with feeling valued by and involved with the organisation, are the key drivers of engagement. They stated that engagement also tends to vary by role. That is, senior managers tend to have the highest levels of engagement (correlating with their high levels of autonomy). Front line people also (despite being fairly junior in hierarchical terms) are highly engaged because of their ability to engage with customers and have an effect on the business at the 'sharp end'. So, being in a back room position, or being 'sandwiched' in a middle management position, can be factors which reduce engagement. For me, this emphasises the fact that you can't take a 'one size fits all' approach to everyone in the organisation.

The question in the mind of you 'cynics' out there will be, is all this just more opinion? Or is it evidence based research? As I have already said, the empowerment era of the 1980s has faded, and a lot of 'engagement' debate has been opinion based. Some recent research by Gallup, (an organisation whose methods and data I respect), has found that employees with the highest levels of commitment, will perform at 20% above the norm, and will be 87% less likely to leave than the norm. This is significant evidence, and persuaded me to use Gallup to measure Asda performance in the area of culture, relative to profit and loss account data. More of that later in this book. People who visited Asda talked about 'the buzz'. The workplace, at both store level and Asda house in Leeds, had a real sense of 'happening', there was excitement and energy. I would suggest that this was because people were committed to Asda, and wanted to satisfy Asda's customers.

This whole subject has risen up the agenda of many CEOs in recent years, but has been plagued by too much 'waffle' and a lack of hard data. McKinsey produced some very interesting 'evidence' in their quarterly review in 2006. It was entitled 'managing your organisation by the evidence'. They looked at 100,000 questionnaires, tracking practises and outcomes, concluding that:

- o 'Carrot and stick' incentives appear to be the least effective of the 4 options commonly used to motivate and encourage employees to perform well and and stay with the company (Herzberg was pretty sure of that conclusion in the 1950s)
- o Key performance indicators, applied in isolation are among the least satisfactory options for increasing accountability (I talked earlier of Asda's balanced use of measures and motivation) (McGregor would say KPIs are theory X management)
- o Relying on a strategy and plan is not the most fruitful way to set a company direction.
- o Command & control leadership (FW Taylor inspired) - still the popular art of telling people what to do and then checking up on them to see that they did it – is amongst the least effective ways to direct the efforts of an organisation's people. (This was proved to me when Asda moved away from traditional command/control management style – so I absolutely concur with the McKinsey research on this)

McKinsey carried out some earlier research in 2004, looking at 180 companies and 24,000 respondents, of whom 11,000 were directors. Their conclusion was that effective management did improve business performance, whilst command and control style was a strong negative. They also found consensus around the fact that the key drivers of 'engagement' were empowering and involving people in decision making. However, the fact remains that although many company boards intellectually believe that engagement is a key area, they are not acting on that belief because they don't really understand what it means in practice. Their intellectual 'buy in' has not resulted in real action or traction in many cases.

Price Waterhouse Coopers also concur that there is no hard evidence, either in the US or in western Europe, that many companies are making real progress on the human capital drivers (leadership; engagement; talent management; innovation) as they define them. PwC suggest (in their report: key trends in human capital 2008) that engagement is a popular management topic. They assert that research has shown a link between a highly engaged workforce and bottom line results, together with the close relationship between employee engagement and customer satisfaction. The theory, in the view of PwC, continues to outdistance the practice.

Despite the fact that employees are beginning to grasp the importance of employee engagement, a survey carried out by the Chartered institute of personnel & development (CIPD) in 2006 'how engaged are British employees', found that only 3 in 10 employees are engaged in their work. For me, that was not a surprising finding. I often ask audiences this question: "how come such a large retail business like Asda, paying not that much more than minimum wage, could win the Sunday Times survey of employees as Britain's best employer in 2002, and be in the top 50 for 5 years? One reason is that so few companies have been working on engagement, or as I prefer to call it – creating a high performance culture.

Price Waterhouse Coopers developed a set of metrics, following the work of professor Stephen Ackroyd of Lancaster business school. Their conclusion was that gaining and maintaining employee engagement is a long term investment, requiring sensitive leadership, and a high degree of respect for individual motivation. I would agree with these conclusions. This is not a quick short term play, nor is it a one size fits all play. I have always said, you need to get to know individuals really well to unlock their motivation and discretionary effort.

So, if there is the emergence of real evidence that high performance is out there to be had, and boards are beginning to get interested, why don't we have a definitive theory of high performance as the leading 'revelation' of the 21st Century? In answer to this question, I love Julia Kirby's article in Harvard business review from July/August 2005. She quotes the working paper of Clay Christensen of Harvard business school and Paul Carlile of Boston university who wrote: "management fads are often created when a researcher studies a few successful companies, finds that they share certain characteristics, concludes that he has seen enough, and then skips the categorisation step entirely by writing a book, asserting that if all managers would imbue their companies with the characteristics of these successful companies, they will be similarly successful."

Kirby states that research is getting better, and that we've come a long way since the early days of Tom Peters 'In search of excellence' and 'cool' companies. I share Kirby's view that everything has to be evidence based. Having a theory is insufficient. Equally, knowing the theory is not sufficient. A great leader has to be able to deliver a high performance culture, and that is an altogether more challenging prospect. Where do you start? What do you need to do? Looking back on the enormous successes with people and high performance at Asda, during my 15 years there, I have noted seven principles which I think made the most material difference to the culture. These were not devised beforehand as part of a blueprint, but have emerged post the changes which revolutionised the Asda culture, and made it such a key component of business performance. I know you will find these seven principles simple, practical and informative. I also believe that you can harness them to improve your performance.

As you begin to read the seven principles of building a high performance culture, you will see some commentary from what I have termed the Asda 'alumni'. These are key individuals who have been senior in the leadership of the Asda business, but who are no longer part of Asda. I have always taken the view that your leavers form your 'alumni', and I wanted to introduce some commentary from those significant senior individuals about the seven principles. I believe that those looking back from the outside of Asda can give a very objective view, since they are not on the payroll. I think you will find their comments illuminating. Details of those individuals are included in Appendix 5.

CHAPTER 5

Principle 1 Hiring for attitude – training for skill

"I am a sociable worker"

Brendan Behan
Irish Playwright 1923 - 1964

This is the first of my seven principles of building a high performance culture, because I believe it is the most important. Hiring is your bedrock. Who you hire into your business is the biggest statement you ever make to your existing people, about the kind of values & standards you hold dear, and where your culture is going.

If people see new recruits and think they are poor calibre/not bright enough/a little weird/don't fit in, or perhaps worst of all are arrogant and try to push people around, it makes a very powerful and bad statement about you and your business. If on the other hand, the individual walks in the door and everyone says "wow", you are making an equally powerful positive statement. Even more so, if they are better than the current calibre, then subliminally everyone begins to think about 'raising their game'. Someone who is bright/enthusiastic/fits well with those around them and gets things done, will be instantly recognised as having high potential, and this says something about the whole workplace being one which is 'going somewhere'.

We all want good people around us. It makes us feel energised, and it makes good things happen. Good people naturally produce good outcomes.

One of the classic traps in hiring is to look for expertise, and to ignore 'fit'. Perhaps the best analogy I can give is the teaching profession (forgive me those of you who teach... I'm sure you are one of the 'good guys' if you are reading this book!). We have all been taught by a few really great teachers who inspired us. We have probably also been taught by someone incredibly bright, no doubt with impeccable academic qualifications, but they just couldn't put it across. Either their communication skills were poor, or they just couldn't control the class. If you hire purely for skill, then this poor result is a potential outcome. In customer facing roles you need to hire someone with good interpersonal and relational skills. It's really critical to success.

Fit with the culture is so important. If you are not very careful, you will hire 'organisational terrorists'. We've all met them, and no doubt spent some of our career working alongside them. Those people who do not 'fit' can spend a lot of time damaging the fabric and belief set of your business. They are corrosive to your high performance culture.

Asda spent 15 years hiring for attitude and training for skill on the shop floor. Asda didn't really care whether people had previous retail experience or not. In fact, retail experience with the wrong attitude was probably the worst combination to hire.

Asda is the only business I know which spent a half day running assessment centres for shop floor people. Many businesses run assessment centres for their graduate scheme, or for management positions, but I know of no one who invests so much time and effort for the shop floor entry to the business. 'Asda magic' is the title of this book, and is also the name of the recruitment process which Asda used for all shop floor selection. It was interactive, and designed to be fun. The process was designed to select people who would enjoy conversation with customers. Asda looked for gregarious people, those with an outgoing personality who enjoy interacting with the public. It is my contention, that you can run as many expensive and high profile customer service programmes as you like, but they will not move your business forward if you are working on the wrong 'raw material', in terms of the personality traits of your new recruits.

Learning most retail skills takes a matter of a few weeks, but having the right personality is vital for enduring business success. Sitting on a supermarket checkout for 4 hours at a stretch can be very repetitive as a task in isolation. But if the checkout operator is gregarious naturally, they will chat to customers as a matter of 'who they are' as a person – because it is part of their personality and 'make up'. That then becomes the recurring satisfaction of the job – giving great service with personality.

I know this has worked for Asda as a business, because the Asda service perception scores told me that

Asda's service was more warm and friendly than all key competitors. Asda also did well on many other performance measures within the area of customer perception. This was no accident. It was about hiring for attitude... then training for skill. The perception data was surveyed every month, by interviewing real customers of all major retail competitors, and was an objective measure of Asda's success over time.

Not only did Asda have quantitative evidence, there was also qualitative evidence of success. Regular customer listening groups asked customers what they thought about Asda and the three things customers always told Asda that it was famous for were price/value, warm friendly service and George clothing. That statement of three from customers appeared uniquely, every time the question was asked over a period of years.

This is evidence of 'Asda magic' at work. Customers cited examples of individuals who represented that reality for them. I remember a letter from an Asda customer who had two children with 'special needs'. She went through the checkout, and the Asda colleague chatted with her, making a special 'fuss' of the children. The customer was so impressed; she felt she had to write in to tell Asda how powerful that experience was. I'm sure the checkout operator thought nothing of it. She was working for Asda, using her normal outgoing gregarious personality. It is a real positive 'virtuous circle', when the individual 'fits' the values of the business, they enjoy their job, and it shows in the service they give. This in turn is noticed by customers, builds loyalty, and also return business.

I often quote my wife in the context of great Asda service. She could have shopped in a number of stores in the Leeds area, but chose to shop in a particular Asda store. She shopped on various days of the week, but always went through the checkout of a particular Asda colleague. She would even join a longer queue to go through her checkout, or queue when other operators were free, because this lady was so friendly and chatty. It made my wife's day. This was 'Asda magic' in action. My wife was not alone in her experience. Many Asda customers told me exactly the same story, when I listened to them in customer listening groups over many years.

Businesses face service 'moments of truth' every day, by their thousands. Whether you take your car in for a service, you go to a retail store, or whether you buy insurance via a call centre. Service 'moments' occur when management are not around, and only the employee and the customer are interacting. In these 'moments of truth', people are the only enduring source of competitive advantage between different providers.

We can all relate bad service experiences. My favourite story is about going into a restaurant in Leeds one evening after work. My wife had been shopping and we met up for a quick meal to save us cooking after a busy day. We went into the restaurant, whose doors were open, to find the waiters for that evening having a meal together. One of them came over and said the fateful words "I'm sorry, we're not open yet, can you come back in 10 minutes?" He wasn't rude, but he missed an opportunity. We didn't come back, we walked for 2 or 3 minutes to another restaurant which was open. We had a better meal, and have never been back. Not only did that employee lose the sale, he lost a customer for good. What he should have done was to say "I'm sorry we're not open yet, but do take a seat and have a look at the menu; someone will be over to serve you in a few minutes". On that basis, we would have remained and continued using that restaurant. Significantly, I have told that story hundreds of times... people are far more likely to give voice to a bad service story, than a good one. By the way, that restaurant closed some 12 months later! I was not surprised.

In my view, people are the only enduring source of competitive advantage. Most everything else is copyable, be it buildings; products or technologies. But people can make the effectiveness of your business very different – positively or negatively.

BUSINESSES WHO DEPLOY THIS EXACT SAME STRATEGY OF HIRING FOR ATTITUDE AND TRAINING FOR SKILL
- *South West Airlines based in Texas – look for 'outrageously' good customer service skills rather than experience. They hire for attitude and train for skill. The only exception is the pilots – they need people who can also fly the planes as well as give good service! They look for a warrior spirit in people who will work very hard and have the will to win. They search for a fun loving attitude which doesn't take itself very seriously, and they look for a servant heart with no ego, which puts*

> *others first. Ego is something not required at Southwest.*
> * *Nordstrom the US department store – look exclusively for people who can be 'nice' to customers. Their line managers and recruiters give out business cards in restaurants if they get great service, asking those people to call them for a job interview*

I'm sure we can all point to examples of 'organisational terrorists'. Those people who dislike, or in some cases even hate, the businesses they work for. They provide a sour note. They affect others and they taint the experience of new hires. Most especially, they kill repeat business in those 'moments of truth' with customers. Hiring for attitude is so critical; because you are searching for the opposite of organisational terrorists... you are looking for brand advocates.

One of the things I like to do when speaking about my experience of the culture change at Asda, is to talk about real people. It's great to understand concepts, but nothing brings a concept to life better than a real example.

Let me talk to you about an Asda colleague I met in an Asda store in North London. I walked into the store to find him working as a greeter, talking to customers as they came into the store. He was very good at it. There was a bit of the 'Asda magic' about him. I was intrigued by his general demeanour, and as I began to talk to him, I realised he was employed because of a people strategy I had introduced some years earlier.

Let me deviate to explain the context of my story. I had been looking at the UK population demographics back in the late 1990's, and realised that with birth rate decline, we needed to open our minds to new sources of recruitment. This was before we saw the large scale of immigration from eastern Europe which subsequently took place.

Based on the data I was looking at then, I decided we should have a concerted 'push' at employing people aged 50 and over. These were people who other businesses (apart from perhaps B&Q) were largely ignoring, and it was long before age legislation gave such people protection from being rejected out of hand. I decided Asda should experiment with this concept, when opening a new store in Broadstairs, Kent. This was the perfect location, a town with a substantive 'retirement community' which would have a high density of the type of people in the target group, and also the Asda colleagues hired would mirror the community in which they worked. When I told the store manager, appointed to open Broadstairs store, that we wanted him to open the store with 50% of his people 50 years old and over, it is fair to say that he was not overjoyed. As I recall, the conversation went along the lines "But David, retail is a young person's game. It's hard work. These older people will be slower, they won't be as productive, and they will take more absence." In the end, he accepted the challenge, and the store opened with 49% of its people aged 50 and over, a pretty good result for a guy who hadn't really wanted to do it.

6 months later, I received a call from the store manager in Broadstairs. He had the good grace to apologise for

his reluctance to hire older workers a year earlier. He told me that many of the young people and students he had originally hired had left the business. However, the over 50's were all still employed. He had found them just as productive; they were not taking absence; and he then told me about an added bonus. He had hired older people with a lot of life skills; they were consequently giving great customer service. What's more, they were so delighted to be considered for employment, when no one else would even interview them that they felt they owed a debt of gratitude to Asda. Based on the experience of Broadstairs Asda adopted the over 50's recruitment strategy for the whole chain.

> *Did you know – Asda was the largest employer of workers aged over 50 in Britain?*

Back to my story.

The greeter in north London was one of the over 50 recruits. He was an industrial chemist by profession, but had been made redundant in his early 50's, because the business where he worked closed down. Sadly, in the year the business where he worked disappeared, he became a widower. He certainly wasn't short of money, because he had a good occupational pension, but he was bored and a little lonely. As we stood talking in the store entrance, he told me that Asda was the only company in the town prepared to give him an interview. He was so delighted to be working for Asda, and he thoroughly enjoyed the human contact of meeting customers. He was motivated by gratitude in joining the Asda family, and in turn Asda had hired a man with tremendous life skills... a professional greeting customers, and taking a great pride in his role. Asda hired for attitude... and what a great hire he was.

Let me also tell you about Stella from the midlands. Stella is another example of hiring for attitude. Stella worked in the George department. At her store she was a fantastic trainer of other colleagues; gave great service to customers and had a very positive outlook on life. Stella also brought one of her neighbours to work daily... she cared very much about others. Despite being a small lady of slight build, Stella was renowned for apprehending shoplifters, and in all the years she worked for Asda, Stella never had a single day off work.

I celebrated Stella's service on stage at one of Asda's store manager Christmas conferences, and she received a standing ovation. A thoroughly genuine, lovely lady. The sort you would call 'salt of the earth'. She was hired because of great attitude, and she was a great fit with the culture of high performance.

Another great illustration of how hiring for attitude produces astonishing customer service concerns a colleague working on the George department in an Asda store in Yorkshire. She observed a male customer looking for a pair of formal black trousers. She went over to offer assistance, because he clearly wasn't able to find his size on the rail. She asked what he wanted the trousers for (she talked to the customer naturally because she had been hired for her gregarious outgoing personality) and he told her they were being purchased for his daughter's Christening service. She knew then that this pair of trousers was important to the customer. Since the correct size was not on the shop floor, she offered to look in the warehouse. Having failed there, she came back to apologise, and since she was unable to order stock into store, she offered to ring other local Asda stores to ascertain whether any of them had the trousers in the right size. She rang five stores within travelling distance, and none of them had the right size for the customer. You probably feel that her efforts were good customer service, and I would agree that she showed real concern, and offered genuine help within the bounds of possibility. What is truly astonishing customer service, is what happened next. This Asda Colleague, realising the trousers were important, and the customer could not wait, she offered to take them home that evening and shorten them, bringing them back next day. This truly amazing service is not in any manual.............she was hired for attitude, and she cared enough to solve the issue herself. This didn't involve long waiting or reference to management, she just got on and solved the problem. My question for you would be................do you have people in the front line, who are sufficiently switched on to do things which astound the customer? You can imagine what our gentleman who wanted to buy trousers thought about Asda. This sort of service is legendary. Is your service legendary? What are you hiring as your standard?

I asked some of the Asda alumni (these are executives who have worked at the very top of the Asda business, either as chief executive or senior roles ....and who now work elsewhere. They are able to give an outside – in view of Asda which is not tainted by being in post and having to say good things...............to read more about them and their backgrounds see Appendix V) to comment in their own words about the importance of hiring for attitude. They wholeheartedly felt this was a key issue, and one they still uphold in other businesses they have subsequently gone to work in.

'Asda alumni' on hiring for attitude:-

Allan Leighton

"Hiring for attitude is massively important. People can usually do the job. That's not the issue. Whether they can apply their skills will depend upon their attitude."

Richard Baker

"Asda was famous for hiring great people. It was an absolute performance culture. Many businesses talk about it. Asda did it."

Dave Cheesewright

"For me, this is one of the most insightful things Asda has ever done. The key for customers is for people to be friendly and helpful. It's infectious and it's low cost. You can't teach service passion to people, you have to hire the right personality. For management, it all boils down to your values. Asda is a business that does what it says on the tin. That alignment between company and values is all about attitude."

Paul Mason

"I've run some very different businesses, and I used both my Mars and Asda experience in order to hire for attitude. You have to assess whether your team has the right attitude to get the job done."

> ### Tony De Nunzio
> "Asda had an absolute focus on people which translated into high energy and motivation........and ultimately customer focus."
>
> ### Archie Norman
> "There is a huge reward for creating self esteem. Asda was hiring people who began with low self esteem in many cases, but went on to achieve in the right environment."

I think you get the point being made here. Attitude is a tangible factor in high performance. That doesn't just hold true for shopfloor colleagues either. True, they are a vital component in the 'supply chain' of great customer service. They are the ones responsible for those 'moments of truth' where they are 'one on one' with customers and no one else is around. However, attitude matters when hiring executives also. Southwest Airlines said they didn't hire for skill with the exception being the pilots. They needed people who had the skill to fly the planes. As we go up the hierarchy of the organisation, we all need people who know what they are doing. They may be specialists or generalists with a lot of experience. However, their attitude to others will play a massive role in their success or failure. Asda hired executives who had a 'fit' the culture. People who would listen to others; people who realised great leadership and people skills were important factors in the high performance of the organisation. I will cover the importance of style of management and leadership later in the book, under principle number four.

I like the Disney view on attitude and hiring. They are a huge service organisation, which relies on their ability to deliver on the fantasy of children. Disney believe that there is a direct correlation between people's involvement in the organisation, and their ability to deliver. If Mickey Mouse is caught smoking in public view during a tea break, that actor could shatter a small child's dreams, and ruin a family holiday. Do they hire for attitude? Of course they do. Disney have a firm belief that when your people 'buy in' to what you're trying to do, you don't have to spend hours micro managing them.........they will intuitively do the right thing. I absolutely agree, and that was my experience at Asda.

So, my first principle of driving a high performance culture is...............to get the right raw material to work with, or you won't get off first base. It sounds really simple, yet so many businesses get this simple part wrong.

Summary points – hire for attitude – train for skill

- Fit trumps skills
- Don't hire organisational terrorists
- Great people will give great customer service
- Great people will always do the right things

Your action notes
Hiring for attitude – training for skill

Based upon what I have read I will... (Go on: do something about it!)

So... what went wrong?
Hiring for attitude

It is a truism, that whatever process you put in place to achieve something, people will find reasons to go around it. This is often because they don't see the value themselves. Sometimes they may have been recruiting in penny numbers, and didn't think it was worth running the full Asda magic process. Sometimes they struggled to find anyone of the right quality to fill awkward unsocial shift hours. Sometimes, they didn't have their bar set high enough on calibre and standards. Any one of those reasons could cause a breach in the system, and the hire would be made of someone who was not of the right attitude and calibre.

The other basic problem in all hiring decisions is that humans are complex individuals, and we all make occasional mistakes. The humans selecting are only human themsleves. The candidates submitting themselves may be very good at 'play acting' in the process, but turn out to be poor on the job. This has always been a material factor, and will have to be dealt with in any hiring process you invent. No process which makes judgements about people is infallible.

All you can do is keep raising your standards and try to get adherence to a process which you know will work most of the time, if properly applied. In truth, hiring is a regular grind for any business hiring large or small numbers of people.

This doesn't make the hiring decision any less important.......rather the reverse. Even though it's hard to get right, it's still the biggest decision you ever make in impacting business performance. Getting this wrong is a big no-no, and has multiplicative negative outcomes. Everyone sees the error. Bad hires affect the performance of many others they come into contact with on a daily basis, because they think no one in management is competent as a result, and their own effort is lowered. The implication is, when you do make a mistake, remove that person early during probation. Don't think they will come around......it rarely happens.

CHAPTER 6

Principle 2 Communicate / communicate / communicate

"Repetition is the mother of learning"

"A picture is worth 1000 words."

"In a world full of audio visual marvels, may words matter to you, and be full of music."
Godfrey Smith

"Don't quote Latin, say what you have to say, then sit down."
Duke of Wellington (on speaking in Parliament)

"Speech is civilisation itself. The word, even the most contradictory word, preserves contact."
Thomas Mann

"I wish people who had trouble communicating would just shut up."
Tom Lehrer

"Words are, of course, the most powerful drug used by mankind."
Rudyard Kipling

Communication is not a 'natural' act. You may find that a strange statement, but 99% of communication misfires.

Let me tell a story against myself to illustrate this. When I was People Director at Asda, we ran a 2 day induction for new management hires in Asda House on a monthly basis, under a programme called 'best welcome'. My role over a number of years was to close the programme. I tried very hard to bring some drama, impactful content and inspiration. My closing session always received good feedback from the new managers attending. I would always say to my audience... "you will forget most of the content of what I'm talking about today, no matter how good/interesting you think it is... but there is one challenge I want to leave with you". I thought that was a pretty impactful line – designed to get them to sit up and take notice. Having issued the challenge, I often asked them to repeat it to me, and then I got them to commit to it. Sounds good, but it was not!

The problem was (and I'm a pretty dynamic/ impactful presenter), that life is busy, and full of other communications constantly hitting people all the time. You are communicating against the background of last night's TV; what's being talked about in their family; a thousand text messages sent and received; mobile phone calls; blog chat; social networks; today's newspaper; today's news news; and 1001 things needing to be remembered at work. You are talking to easily distracted, 'busy traffic' butterfly brains... most of the time. That's the reality. All business communication has to compete with 'noise'.

To finish my story, I realised the impact of talking to 'busy minds' when I bumped into a couple of young Asda graduates in the Asda Wembley store of learning. They had been at my 'best welcome' closing speech. They told me how much they loved working for Asda and what a great experience 'best welcome' had been. The conversation was going really well, until I asked if they remembered my session. "Yes" they said "it was really good". However, it was red faces all around when I asked if they could remember my one challenge they had committed to. Of course they couldn't. I had communicated that once, to very busy people, and they had quickly forgotten it.

Why did we learn multiplication tables 'by wrote' when I was in primary school? Because it sticks. I don't think they teach that way any more, but I never have any trouble remembering my multiplication tables. I've never forgotten the Lord's prayer from school assembly either! Repetition is clearly the mother of all learning.

To be an effective communicator, you have to communicate – communicate – communicate. It has to become a mantra... a way of life for you, every single day.

So many times in my career, I have heard people say "I sent a note out on that". Today people tend to tell you the information has been placed on the company intranet. However, the bad news is, that isn't good communication. If you send something out once, and follow it up again, and speak to people via a TV video message, and you get your local management to brief the same thing on a number of occasions regularly... then you might start to get some of your messages through.

Send one message in isolation... and you have absolutely no chance of getting through to people... you may as well not have bothered.

People are constantly busy, and we all skim read. We take in headlines, and if something attracts, we may take in a little more. We take more information from pictures than written words... television has conditioned us all that way, but pictures have always been powerful purveyors of information. That phrase 'a picture is worth 1000 words' is a truism.

Asda tried very hard over the years to use the learning from tabloid newspapers in communication techniques. That is not because Asda thought people were stupid... it was because there was real recognition about the way in which people digest information. People look at pictures, scan headlines and assimilate a few simple top line facts. Very few approach the world by reading in detail every single line of information. The brain just wouldn't cope with that sort of processing. We take an approach which 'sifts information' and uses just what we need.

This led Asda to an approach which always sought to use plain simple English. In every communication people attempted to use "Daily Mirror" speak (apologies to both the Mirror and any of the other tabloid newspapers who might be offended by omission). This was a helpful shorthand to remind communicators to make communication short, snappy and eminently readable.

Asda began to have complex documents vetted and simplified by people like "clear as a bell" all in a major drive to be clear and easy to understand. We all get an immediate sense, as the receiver of a communication, about what is being said when it is kept simple.

When businesses are talking about complex matters such as pensions or share option schemes, there is a huge propensity to launch into complex quasi legal speak, with more caveats and jargon than you can shake a stick at. With pension or share scheme documentation, Asda used pictures/cartoons/simple language; all in an attempt to get the message home. Rest assured, people will only read documents if you have gone to these kind of lengths.

> *I admire other businesses who work hard at pictorial communication. John Timpson, chairman of Timpson; the key cutting/watch and shoe repair business, has spent much of his business life drawing cartoons for his many 'in house' books and magazines. They are humorous and instantly help to get across the points he wishes to make to his people. His work is excellent, and well worth a look if you want to observe excellence in written communication in action.*

I have always said that the cultural change at Asda was communication led. Many change programmes are development led. The normal observable pattern is that a guru runs a 'cascade' programme, and everyone is supposed to get on board. At Asda, the change was much more on a day by day, week by week disciplined basis. Cultural change often fails after short term change/development programmes. My contention, based upon my Asda experience, would be that change underpinned by continuous and effective face to face communication is far more likely to succeed.

To tackle this very issue, Asda began a thing called the daily 'huddle'. This was the intention to give every employee a daily 5/10 minute face to face briefing at shift changeover for teams all around the business. Asda has done this for over 15 years, and such regular and repetitive communication is a hard fought slog. Asda measured the frequency of holding huddles; measured them in Asda's attitude survey called "we're listening", and performance in holding effective huddles was discussed at just about every major management conference. I opened this chapter by stating that communication is not a natural act. What I mean by that, is that you have to work really hard at it if you want to improve the performance of your business.

The problem is, businesses get very busy with the day to day activities, and other random things also crowd in. In a typical retail day, thousands of small activities need to be accomplished. However, there is a real power in getting your team together at the start of their shift, to brief them and get some quick feedback. Time spent doing this task effectively will help speed up every other task in the day. World class communication, encompassing an effective daily briefing, is a 'magic ingredient' in your culture.

Asda spent time telling all colleagues 'what's going on/how the business was doing/what needs doing today, and listened to any issues of the day coming back from people in the business.

> *This is not rocket science. The Industrial Society (now known as the Work Foundation) sought to push the concept of "team briefing" in the 1970's as a best practice for British business... so the concept is nothing new.*

I found that because Asda told it like it was, 'warts and all', colleagues in the business were really motivated and engaged as a consequence. Most retailers traditionally have not told their people about sales (they might leak the figures to the competition) or the profits (they might want more money) and they certainly didn't air their issues/problems to the wider team. Asda's belief was exactly the opposite of this. My personal view is very clear, the more people know, the more they will care.

Asda was not the only business to major on this principle of honesty and openess. I was in a US Nordstrom department store, and watched the store manager there running their morning 'rally' (which was very similar to an Asda 'huddle'). The briefing was all about sales figures for the previous day, service feedback from customers, and the whole event was designed to motivate. There was theatre, there was celebration, there was 'atmosphere'. Employees had those large plastic 'hand clappers' to make 'noise' when someone was being recognised. The whole 'rally' was led by the store manager, and she was a professional communicator. A great example of my principle communicate/communicate/communicate at work in a world class retailer.

Similarly, Ritz Carlton, the high end hotel chain, also holds what they call a 'line up'. Everyone employed in teams in the hotel chain, is briefed daily about the special requirements of guests, and any issues of the day. Ritz Carlton's view is that they couldn't offer a 5 star service without that level of constant daily communication with their people.

To give you an example of the effect of what I'm talking about, in 2007 I visited one of Asda's stores in Alloa. I was in a large group of colleagues in a 'listening group' (people gathered from the shop floor to give me feedback as a Director of the business), and we ranged around a number of topics they wanted to discuss. I asked them about the effectiveness of communication and the quality of daily 'huddles' in their store. They said "we've never worked in a business which has told us so much. We feel really involved with the store".

A few years earlier, Asda had opened a store in Blackwood in the valleys of South Wales. A lot of the colleagues Asda employed had previously worked in factories of various sorts, many in the textile industry. Again the reaction listening to colleague opinions in that store was the same "we're amazed by how well communicated with we are. It makes us feel motivated. We think Asda is a great business to work for". There is a direct link between feeling 'in the loop' about what is going on in the business and high levels of engagement and the resulting high performance of people.

Both those stores have morale indices in the 90's, and both give great service to their customers based on perception data at those two units. They illustrate the principle of communicate/communicate/communicate; 'the more you know, the more you care'. I have spent time in my retail career asking shop floor colleagues about communication effectiveness, and this point about the need to feel 'in the loop' has come back to me time and time again. I passionately believe in good communication. You have to make sure people understand why something is happening. This is the key to motivation and engagement.

If you are told to do something, you may do it, or you may not. You may reluctantly do it, but not brilliantly. However, if someone takes time to explain why you are being asked to do something; they explain both the problem and the situation; they help you see the evaluation of options and how important it is for customers that the issue is fixed. Then you are much more likely to do what is being asked of you. But, more importantly, you are likely to do it with real enthusiasm... you feel you 'own' the solution....which is that bit of Asda magic 'fuel' for gaining high performance.

Most Asda colleagues knew that Asda had won the Grocer 33 (33 items surveyed by test purchase, by the Grocer magazine, to benchmark supermarket prices....... across a basket of staple items shopped weekly) for 13 years, proving Asda had the lowest basket price of any of its competitors. Asda wanted colleagues to talk to customers about that substantial achievement. Telling them the facts just wasn't enough. When I was in store with a bunch of colleagues, one of my favourite exercises was to ask them what they knew about Asda's price position. Most would say Asda was the cheapest. "Yes, but how do you know?" was my second question. Some

ASDA MAGIC

would say they knew because they did their shopping with Asda and it was good value. I tended to then retort with "yes, but how do you know?"

After a while of thinking, someone in the group would say "Asda have won the Grocer 33 for 13 years". I would then ask my next question "what is the Grocer 33?" This was usually the point where any group of colleagues would begin to look at each other for a clue, because they didn't usually know the answer. They might know that 'the Grocer' was a magazine, but they tended to guess that it was a monthly publication rather than a weekly (it comes out weekly). I would ask them how the Grocer assessed who was the cheapest retailer. They tended to guess that the Grocer magazine went to hundreds or even thousands of stores to look at prices. When I told them that the the the staff of the magazine went to one store of each of the main grocers each week... maybe a J Sainsbury in Scotland; a Tesco in London; a Morrison's in South Wales; an Asda in Cornwall etc, they began to understand the mechanics of the survey, and it became real for them. "Do they do a shop?" someone would usually ask me, and I confirmed that they did. We would talk through the fact that the Grocer survey bought 33 items each week in each of the main retailers, always the basics such as bread and milk, but also changing seasonal items such as fruit, salads and barbeque in summer or soups and potatoes in winter. When colleagues understood the mechanics of the survey, and the fact that Asda might lose one week because of a couple of deep cut promotions in the basket in Morrison's, but that overall Asda won more weeks every year than any other retailer, their confidence in talking to customers increased massively. This is the power of understanding in good communication. It motivates and engages people. It's not just a fact download, but a proper adult dialogue. The proper explanation... done in the style of a question and answer session was much more powerful than just the bare facts. Colleagues wanted to go out of the meeting room and tell their workmates; they wanted to tell their families, they wanted to tell their customers. Good communication causes a real buzz in your business... it produces ownership and action. Try it for yourself... you might be surprised by a bit of that magic and its power in your own business!

Let's hear from the Asda alumni about communicating:-

Paul Mason
"You get people to follow you by communication. The best piece of communication I remember in Asda was the creation of the strapline 'No2 by 2002' to overtake J Sainsbury. It was digestible at all levels. The communication issue sits with the sender. In Levi's, I had an international European board. You really have to verify that communication has been received. We had to create very simple messages that could be elaborated across countries."

Justin King
"There was a belief in Asda that people need to know what is expected. People are more likely to do a good job if they know what you need to achieve and why. Communications are such an important part, and moreso the larger the business entity. Communication

---

is hard work, you have to be relentless. There must be great processes in the business."

Dave Cheesewright

"At Asda, repetition was institutionalised as the queen of learning. We gave out the same messages 3 or 4 times every Monday for onward cascade. Repetiton gives clarity and explains the context. I have taken Asda's 'huddles' to the Wal-Mart business in Canada."

Allan Leighton

"Asda was famous for the set piece communications: the daily 'huddle'; the store manager quarterly meetings; The 'late lunch'. None of these happened by accident, and they were all designed to ensure no one didn't feel they could play a part in driving the business forward."

Richard Baker

Conferences at Asda were always 'electric'. The mechanisms for communication were world class, and years ahead of everyone else. Most businesses still haven't got there. There was a lot of plain speaking, direct, face to face, with 'jolly' but serious messages. The 'huddle' apparatus was 20 years ahead of its time."

Archie Norman

"A lot of people thought the communications were gimmicks. You should not be famous for the way you broadcast. It was all about what was 'behind' the message. Sometimes the Asda story gets distorted. It shouldn't be about the personality, but about the what."

I think you begin to get the picture. I have repeated this point about communication over and over again, because great communication is one of my personal passions. It's just so vitally important in creating the 'magic'. It is a foundation principle of a high performance culture. Without this, your business cannot effectively thrive. The CEO must be the chief communicator and keep at it 'ad nauseum'. How would you rate your business on a scale of 0-10, on the effectiveness of your internal communications? Do you switch off the people who feel 'out of the loop', or do you engage all of your people by putting a lot of effort into keeping the' in the loop'?

Summary points – communicate / communicate / communicate

- o Culture change should be communications led
- o Use plain, simple language / pictures / cartoons
- o A good picture is worth 1000 words
- o We live in a soundbite world – learn to use soundbites brilliantly
- o Snappy / buzzy / quick daily briefings are the way to energise a successful business
- o Communication is your business life blood
- o Inspire as you communicate – it's a massive opportunity
- o The more they know – the more they will care!

Your action points – communicate / communicate / communicate

Based upon what I have heard, in the context of communicating, I am going to...

Remember... you will be spending time and money on communications at present. Evaluate... every document, every memo, every briefing in your business. That evaluation may surprise you.

So... what went wrong?
Communicate / communicate / communicate

Despite the fact that I have said that I believe the cultural revolution at Asda was communication led, that doesn't mean that I believe the business achieved the quest for some 'holy grail'. Communication is an unnatural act. People's attention is diverted by so many things.

Asda struggled daily to make communications short; simple and punchy. Asda struggled constantly to reach everyone every day. Some managers simply were not inspiring in their delivery, and information came across in a very mechanical and monotonous way. Checkout colleagues were continually serving customers, and consequently were particularly hard to brief effectively, because there was no common downtime in the shift. You cannot stop the checkout bank to hold a briefing. Customers wouldn't be happy with that!

Despite those issues, what I do know, is that this daily struggle was worth the fight. Great communication does affect business performance positively. It's just tough to do it well, and to do it consistently. Any business which wants a high performance culture will have to grapple with human inadequacy and inconsistency. It's part of the struggle in which all businesses and organisations are engaged. Sometimes you just have to have the perseverance, grit and determination to push through.

CHAPTER 7

Principle 3 Listening

> "Our best ideas come from clerks and shop floor associates"
>
> Sam Walton
> Founder of Wal Mart
>
> "It is the province of knowledge to speak, and the privilege of wisdom to listen."
>
> Oliver Wendell Holmes
>
> "A good listener is not someone who has nothing to say. A good listener is a good talker with a sore throat."
>
> Katherine Whitehorn

I often say that God gave us one mouth and two ears, and we should operate in that sort of ratio! A lot of managers operate like 'motor mouth'; they never seem to stop talking. There seems to be an enormous propensity to love the sound of your own voice. I suppose this is partly a function of ego, and partly a 'learned' management behaviour, which holds to the view that the one who gives the most input will rise to the top, or their view will prevail. My view on this would be that we all do too much talking and too little listening. I have always been a good listener. People tell me that. I am a 'baby boomer' from the generation when children were told they should be 'seen and not heard'. I was also an only child, and therefore was surrounded by adult conversation. Apparently I talked very early in life, and developed an adult vocabulary. I learned by listening. Using adult vocabulary was something I found useful in bringing up my own children a generation later. Never underestimate the intelligence or language capabilities of a child. Give them big words and adult concepts early, and they will surprise you!

Anyway, this is not a book about parenting, so lets return to the point in hand.....listening. Listening is something we have a tendency to do too little of, as managers and leaders. However, properly used, it is another of those 'magic' ingredients which made Asda a success story. Asda elevated listening into an 'art form'. Listening Groups were conducted with colleagues around the business on a regular basis. Store managers were charged with holding listening groups on a regular basis. Asda also conducted listening groups with customers regularly and systematically. A programme called 'be a shopkeeper', was introduced, to ensure managers from the head office worked with colleagues on the shopfloor, and got close to what they did. It was a very effective way to listen to their operational concerns and feedback. A programme called 'be a customer', similarly was about holding regular listening groups with customers; packing bags for them on the checkouts, and accompanying them around the store while they shopped. This gave invaluable insight into their thinking, and found out their views on the business. Over time, Asda became famous for listening to colleagues on how the business was run, and thereby getting them involved in actioning matters pertaining to morale (communication / training / leadership behaviour etc.) via a concept called 'colleague circles'. Every store / distribution centre and office in the business formed a colleague circle from volunteers at that place of work, and they became vibrant guardians of the changing culture.

Like many businesses, Asda also conducted a regular attitude and engagement survey. There is nothing unusual in that. However, the point of difference was that although each workplace had only one survey per year, Asda was running that survey in 10/12 stores/locations around the business every single week of the year, on a rolling basis.

That meant that during my time as people director for Asda, I had continuous weekly 'radar' on how people were feeling about the business as a whole; training and development; communications; their manager or leader; pay and benefits... those things which really matter to people. I couldn't have done my job without knowing those things intimately.

To have regular rolling feedback means, in effect you are always systematically listening. As well as answering the survey questions, colleagues had opportunity to give free flow comments about the best and worst things about the business, and reading such feedback gave any reader priceless access to information. That regular barometer of attitude and engagement is another piece of the 'Asda magic'. I commend readers to compare this with the more typical annual 'organisational indigestion' of a massive survey of all employees all at the same moment in time.

If the leader is armed with such closeness to 'how your people feel', it means that no one can ever surprise you. From inception in the early 1990's, Asda continually amended and 'tweaked' the questions asked in the attitude survey (known as "we're listening") In 2008 the question count was taken down from over 50 to only 14, in order to make it easier for a fast moving retail business, (with 175,000 people), to complete it. Asda achieved participation and completion rates of 99 percent, which is no mean feat... and way above any other business I have ever quizzed about attitude survey response rates.

The high participation in the survey was in no small part down to being run and administered by the 'colleague circles' I mentioned earlier. They often used a prize draw in their place of work to encourage completion, which adds some reward for doing the inputting.The survey was on screen online, to assist the efficiency of collating and distributing the results. Colleagues over the years also grew to trust the total anonymity of the survey. No individual could be traced as to what responses were given, or what was said.

I am delighted to say that the engagement results from those early days in the 1990's to 2009 grew from very mediocre initially, to an overall cumulative index for the Asda business of 92%. 93% of Asda's colleagues thought that Asda was a 'great place to work' and 96% enjoyed working for Asda. Such results were consistent, and the trend improved year on year over 15 years. It was a linear progression during my time in the business.

I think the reader will agree that these are deeply impressive numbers, though no business should ever become complacent, (remember the paranoia I talked of earlier). However, Asda was achieving very good "we're listening" index scores long before Asda was recognised as no. 1 best place to work in the Sunday Times survey. Many people in other businesses have told me they were very surprised to see Asda at the top of the Sunday Times index. Their assumption was that Asda was known as a 'pretty good' employer, with some innovative/zany ideas, and a good reputation for flexible working practices, but they had no idea Asda was that good, especially in comparison to other much smaller businesses. People naturally assumed that a company employing 175,000 people, most of whom were hourly paid shop workers, couldn't possibly compete with small professional service businesses, with a majority of salaried employees. They were wrong in that assumption!

For my part, I enjoyed the participation in the Sunday Times/Financial Times surveys, because those external surveys merely confirmed what was known internally to the business. Asda's internal "we're listening" scores showed employees felt Asda was a great place to work, with some individual workplaces achieving phenomenal levels of engagement.

That is not to say that Asda didn't have some individual stores or distribution centres where there were issues. Nor is it implying that even in good stores Asda didn't have a poor result in one department or on one particular shift. What a survey result does, is allow a management team to respond to that listening data. Because Asda was dealing with results from only 10/12 stores/units at any one time, there was no feedback/listening "indigestion" caused by a surfeit of information. Asda was able to take a view of that microcosm of results, and take action accordingly.

Each colleague circle built up an action plan, based upon their results, in conjunction with the local management team. The power of the listening, therefore, was that it was a local action plan. The magic, was in always keeping the action as close to the listening as possible. Local action plans tend to be more meaningful, and doing something about a local manager running a team who is thought to be bullying or using inappropriate behaviour, means that the whole exercise becomes more credible.

At a company level, Asda also held a "we're listening forum" on a quarterly basis, to examine trends, and take action on emerging patterns. If colleagues didn't like the food in their store restaurants, then the key people who ran that operation could debate this and do something about it. It is said that any 'army' marches on its stomach, so negative feedback on food across a number of locations would be a pretty big deal. If colleagues working on night shifts found their uniforms impractical for replenishing the store shelves overnight, that also would be important to listen to, because it could lower morale and harm productivity. Productivity is a vital feature of any business, but in a people business like retail, where there are very few machines, and lots of people, then morale and productivity are absolutely linked. In such circumstances, feedback about something like a more practical night uniform could be a priority to get sorted.

As an organisation learns to listen and respond in a systematic and organised way, there is a clear impact on engagement and morale. The responding is just as important, if not more so, than the listening itself. Responding doesn't always mean 'doing things' either. People sometimes ask for things that would be wrong for the business, or simply things which the business just couldn't afford to do. Saying "no can do" with a proper explanation as to why (refer back to what I said about telling people why in principle 2 – communicate, communicate, communicate) will more often than not, enhance the respect from those who work for you.

The other strength of responding to Asda engagement surveys was the work of colleague circles and local line managers who worked hard and diligently to follow up and deal with issues arising from the "we're listening" survey. It was those individuals who were a key part of the Asda magic... that localness and closeness to dealing with the issues in the Asda culture thereby making the business better little by little.

"We're listening" was an important key result area for line managers in charge of people during my 15 years in Asda, and this systematic handling of such a key area undoubtedly drove the involvement of colleagues in the Asda business.

When Allan Leighton was Chief Executive of Asda, he used to talk about the power of "listening to the river". I know Allan conducted a lot of systematic listening to 'postie's' when he became chairman of the Post Office. I'm sure he's doing the same thing in Loblaws – the food retail chain in Canada.

Let's hear some commentary from the Asda alumni on the art of listening:-

Tony De Nunzio
"I have instituted a 'make a difference survey' in Maxeda (retail chain in the Netherlands), which replicates Asda's 'we're listening' survey, which is a real temperature check of the culture, and a universal language. From this listening, we are able to address areas for improvement, and benchmark our progress across different areas of the company."

Paul Mason
"Asda had aggressive programmes of listening. I took listening groups into Somerfield with me. Every leader has an ego. Most leaders think they have the answer. If you get the feedback on what is happening, you must allow it to change your view."

Justin King
"The board at Asda used to complain about going out to listen to shop floor colleagues on pay & benefits. But if you do this on a widescale basis, you get a feel for what people think, and people know you've been out there. I do this in

---

J Sainsbury. People know that I'm getting around and listening."

Dave Cheesewright
"Listening to customers and associates is a big deal in the Wal-Mart Canadian business. It is always customers or associates who know how to solve problems. A lot of companies don't tap into this..........but it's just so powerful. Asda came very close to developing a self-sustaining culture of listening. I have taken that with me."

Allan Leighton
"My whole thing is around being out and about. In delivery offices at the Royal Mail, stopping a postie on their round. Out in retail stores, you always learn something. They describe it in their own words, as opposed to 'management speak', and it is much more impactful."

Archie Norman
"I still spend time listening now. It is almost impossible to get some managers to listen. Embracing the front line matters. What they say is just as important as whether they're right or not."

One of the things of real power that was created at Asda was the confidence that colleagues could say what they thought without fear of reprisal. All the companies I talk to have a very strong grapevine, and much of the negativity and frustration comes out by the coffee machine or the water cooler. People in organisations are talking to each other continually, but not necessarily to the leaders who can make change happen. It is much healthier to tell your people that it's OK to air your views in the right way, and be seen to deal with things out in the open.

Some years ago, I took a group of external visitors to a colleague listening group at an Asda store in central London. I told them that our people felt free to comment without fear of reprisal. They were sure that the presence of a few 'suits' at the back of the room would cause suspicion and be inhibitive. I introduced the visitors to the colleagues in the room, and we got into the process of listening to what they had to say. Within seconds, they launched into a very normal free flow of thoughts, ideas and comments about the business... their business. They held nothing back, and it was a great listening session. My guests were amazed at the passion and quality of commentary on the business, and their comment was that "we never normally see this level of immediacy and honesty... it's a wow".

There is real power in feedback which knows there will be no retribution. Asda often used the phrase "feedback is the breakfast of champions", and enlightened leaders believe it is. So often in daily business life, managers tend to tell their leaders the good things; the things which are going well; the things they are proud of. Naturally, managers want to appear competent and on top of things. It's perfectly normal. It doesn't make them bad people. What it does mean, is that a senior leader will have a strange diet of generally positive feedback, and the odd really major problem which comes to them. What will be missed in these circumstances, is a whole tidal wave of minor things which are going wrong in the business, because they are 'below the radar'.

Because Asda sought to energise people and seek their views regularly, they genuinely didn't fear punishment for giving negatives. They gave quality feedback... 'warts and all', there was no 'pulling of the punches'. Leaders really do need to know about those things. Only by finding out what is not working can a leader be genuinely productive, and able to quickly fix and improve business processes.

An example from Disney of fixing an issue based on listening

This story concerns the problem of customers parking in their huge theme parks, unable to find their car. They had tried all sorts of ways to notify people where they were parked, but coming back to acres of vehicles at the end of a long day in a theme park was spoiling the whole experience for many families. Tired customers certainly didn't remember where they had parked in the morning, and roaming round looking for their vehicle was a sour note at the end of the day. Disney asked the students who were working for them, parking the customer vehicles, to come up with a solution to the issue which would work. Their idea was to create a simple map of the car park, and fill it in for the time of day in sections. If you told the attendant roughly what time you had parked, he could then take you directly to the section to locate your vehicle. This was a cheap and effective solution, which came from listening to those close to the issue.

During my Asda career I found the power of listening to be astonishing. Many great ideas which Asda implemented came from listening to shop floor colleagues. Asda became famous for flexible working practices, and many of the schemes the business adopted over the years were suggested by Asda people.

One example of how people from the shop floor produced ideas for flexible working, came from a listening group I was holding with a bunch of colleagues, about the reasons for absence, and what actions the business should be taking to improve absence management in their view. They were a lively group and very engaged with the absence issue. There was no defensiveness, and no fear of reprisal. There was an Asda 'magic moment' in this group. One lady had the courage to say... straight out... "you know David, most of us are mums with young children. Often when we ring in sick, it's not us who are ill, it's our children. Our partners have gone to work, or we are single parents, and we are literally left holding the baby." There was a silence, and a lot of nodding from the colleagues around the room. You know when you have unearthed a nugget! I listened carefully, acknowledged the point, and then asked the $64,000 question "OK, I understand that is a real issue, what should we do about it?" Another colleague in the group then chipped in and proffered the idea... "why don't we share phone numbers in teams, so that we can ring a fellow colleague and organise to swap shifts?"

One thing the reader should understand is that most retail teams are made up of part time workers, with people working generally 3 or 4 different days per week, usually of differing shift lengths. There are some full timers, but they tended to be the minority. The suggestion for a shift swap scheme sounded like a good practical idea for bringing down absence, and I agreed to take it away and look at it. A young male in the listening group also said it would work for more organised things, like big matches or day trips to events.

Asda drafted up and branded the scheme "shift swap", giving colleagues the facility to organise this. On launch, line managers were very wary of the scheme and unsure how/whether it would work. It was, in effect, a removal of their line management 'control'. Asda encouraged them to let this particular control go. The rationale being, "why control who turns up for a shift, as long as someone qualified does turn up"? Better to have someone on the job, than a mum having to lie when she rings in, or a guy not turning up because his football team are playing away.

Once management got used to 'letting go', shift swap became a powerful tool in the Asda armoury around flexible working practices, and absence was reduced as a result. It was a win-win situation. People were delighted their idea had been put into practice, and absence costs were reduced. I claim no credit... it was a fabulous shop floor colleague idea, borne of the honesty of being able to listen without the fear of reprisal... that's magic!

Summary points – listening to 'the river'

- Talk less / listen more
- Create a culture of feedback without fear of reprisal.
- There are things you need to know to drive productivity – is stuff working?
- Your managers want to look good – it's natural – your shop floor feedback can be much more candid
- Make your listening systematic and regular – a way of life for all leaders
- You can't get too much feedback – it is the breakfast of champions

Your action points – listening

How will you become a more systematic listener?

What mechanics will you use to respond to issues you hear about?

So... what went wrong?
Listening

The problem with listening is finding the time to do it regularly, and following through with what you hear. My experience tells me that the majority of people believe in listening, but believing doesn't guarantee action. Asda was a very fast moving 'busy' business. I'm sure that the buyers and traders would have loved to spend more time in the stores listening to colleagues and customers about what their reactions were to new product lines, and general changes being made. However, their key focus was always going to be negotiating and buying those products. I'm sure that the Asda store managers and distribution managers thought it was important to listen to their people and their customers. The trouble is, they also had a very busy and pressurised day job which threatened to steal every hour they had available. There will always be reasons not to listen. I don't think Asda was unique in this. Overcoming the problem is about systematically making time to listen.

The second issue is equally important. Having listened, it is vital to respond. Even if the response is to say 'no', or to explain that what is being asked for is unaffordable or unworkable. People don't like a negative response, but it is far better than the more frequent response... hearing nothing. If you have listening mechanics, without responding, then the dissatisfaction levels will grow. In fact, it will be worse than not listening in the first place.

I can't say that Asda completely solved either of these problems. In a large organisation, they are part of the 'pull and push' of time priorities and resources. However, I believe Asda did much more listening than the average business, and as a consequence moved the scale of engagement and business performance to a higher level.

Chapter 8

Principle 4 Choose your style
of management and leadership

"The Nation had the lion's heart. I had the luck to give the roar"

Winston Churchill (1874-1965)

"The style is the man."

Book of Proverbs – The Bible

"Leadership is the art of accomplishing more than the science of Management says is possible."

General Colin Powell

"Hundreds of books and millions of dollars in consulting fees have been devoted to leadership and organisational change. No issue for the past 15 years has concerned all managers, or a wider spectrum of organisations... The most important things a leader can bring to a changing organisation are passion, conviction and confidence in others... leaders set the direction, define the context, and help produce coherence for their organisation."

Rosabeth Moss Kanter

Too much has been written about management and leadership, as if it were a science rather than an art. I'm not going to attempt to plough through that well worn furrow in any way at all. I'm sure that most of the readers of this book will have some fairly well developed ideas as to what works for them in terms of leadership. My question is does it really work?

> "As a scientific concept, leadership is a mess"
> Augier and Teece 2005

My purpose in thinking about the magic of the Asda culture, is to show how different the developed leadership style became to that of a traditional retail business. I have seen enough of the retail sector to know that the majority of retail businesses are made up of a command and control style structure. They operate in an almost military fashion. Managers and leaders have absolute control, and bark the orders to their workforce, expecting absolute obedience and adherence. Don't get me wrong, this is not an entirely ridiculous approach. You do need a degree of 'military control' in Retail. As a customer, you want to know that all price changes to a product have been enacted properly in store, and even more importantly that new product ranges have been put out on shelf with a degree of military precision.

Asda set out to change from that "tell and do" mentality in the early 1990's. That style of leadership had not produced differentiation from the competition, and after the failure of Asda in the early 1990's, there was a real desire to change the approach, aiming to get more engagement from the workforce. The introduction of the "Asda way of working" was about "getting things done willingly and well, through others". A tell and do style produces a climate of fear and a level of anxiety. Things get done in the short term, but a high proportion of people will leave the business as a consequence of that style. Others will just do the bare minimum required. 'Tell and do' as a style will not tap into the soul, the heart or the spirit of the people in the business.

Real success is about accessing that area of the human spirit which produces outperformance. People can't be told to do it, it can only occur when they want to do it. This is the element of discretionary effort over and above the norm which individuals can give, but collectively causes organisations to outperform.

I like the work on leadership by Kouzes and Posner which talks about modelling the way; inspiring a shared vision and encouraging the heart amongst their key principles. You can read their work in 'the leadership challenge' by James Kouzes and Barry Z Posner. It may add something to your lexicon of leadership beliefs.

Lets hear what some of the Asda alumni have to say about the Asda way of working and the style of management/leadership...

Allan Leighton
"Asda was about tough love. It was all based on respect, since we believed that giving it would pay back over time."

<u>Dave Cheesewright</u>
"Everyone at Asda was interested in what you were good at, and how you could be better. Asda took your strengths and made you stronger. Mars, where I came from, was about identifying your weaknesses and showing you how you could improve. Asda was very competitive, and liked winning. It did this by playing to strengths."

<u>Justin King</u>
"Asda was prepared to be self challenging and harder on itself than others would be. Asda had a 'can do' attitude, and was always clear on what made it different."

<u>Paul Mason</u>
"Leadership is about taking people to a place they wouldn't go on their own. You have to be able to envisage where the business needs to go. Fundamentally, it is about getting people to believe that they can get to somewhere different."

<u>Tony DeNunzio</u>
"Asda had a simple business model about people first; strategy to win second and successful execution third."

The idea of getting people to work with their heart and soul in the workplace, rather than just bringing their arms and legs to work, is extremely powerful. A lot has been written about empowerment, which seems now to have morphed currently into an over use of the word engagement. I often wonder if people are just using buzz words, but don't understand the real essence of what this is all about. Essentially, you have to get your business to a place where all your managers 'get it'. This is not about using buzz words; it is about people working with others and leading them in the right way.

In the early days of Asda's cultural journey, a simple 4 box model was used to describe what was required from leaders.

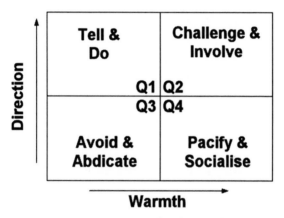

Diagram 4 – Leadership style

The model was there to help leaders understand that a 'tell and do' style may be effective in the short term, and appropriate if you want to evacuate a building in the event of a fire, but involving and challenging people in a different way would tap into a whole source of soul, spirit, strength and initiative that just telling never could. The aim was to move leaders from a predominantly Q1 style to box Q4. This was still giving leadership and direction, but in a much warmer and more involving way. The aim was to take your people with you.

Introducing this methodology, produced some interesting consequences. Some managers were unable to change their overbearing dictatorial style, based on heavy reliance upon hierarchy and position power. Over time, about a third of Asda managers left the business... it was not for them; they weren't for changing, because they were incapable of making that change. They couldn't manage in a different way... they just didn't have the ability or the flexibility....and in some cases they had no intention of changing. It was a case of change the people, or change the people.

About a third of the managers were early adopters of the Asda way of working. They were delighted by the direction and change. They were good people managers already, and consequently understood the potential of leading in this way and taking people with them. The whole style of management was an easy transition for them, and they quickly began to see improved results.

Finally, Asda had to work pretty hard with the middle third of managers. They were in some cases 'pretenders', those who said they were on board, but weren't in reality. Some of them thought they had 'got it' but in practice found it a challenge to operate in that way. Some were just plain confused. They began to soften their style so much that they merely became 'pacifiers' and 'socialisers' (Q3 on the 4 box model). They felt it was all about being a 'nice person' and avoiding conflict. Some managers slipped into 'avoiding' and 'abdicating' their accountability for fear of upsetting their people (Q2 on the 4 box model).

When a business makes a change in style of the magnitude Asda was aiming for, there is a real need to keep showing by example what you mean. You have to have role models; you have to coach the style you want; you have to induct and inculcate your methods… and you have to keep at it.

I have a basic belief in the power and importance of the psycological contract at work. Whether you use the word empowerment or engagement, leadership is about energising people through your leadership style and behaviour. Most people come to work wanting to do a good job. Sadly, it is often their manager who switches them off in some way. Poor management is almost always the reason for every leaver beginning the process of looking for a new job. Leavers may say they are leaving for more money (people rarely leave for less), but the real reason originated with manager behaviour.

Think for a minute about a colleague/boss who loves football. It is not an exclusively male preserve to exhibit this behaviour, but mostly it is guys who do it. I'm sure we've all worked for at least one person in our careers who talks about sport and little else. This tends to focus primarily on football rather than other sports (why is that?… clearly needs to be the subject of some academic study!) and they go on and on. Last nights game is dissected in minute detail; player performance is discussed; opportunities missed are bemoaned; the referee is emasculated; the behaviour of the crowd and the swearing, singing or violence is relived. You have all heard this type of conversation, and I predict two possible reactions. You either love it or you hate it.

Those who love it are immediately the 'in crowd' who add colour from their own comments, or jibes and disdain by supporting another team. Either way, they are into the communication 'channel' with full vigour, and part of 'the team'. However, those who have no interest are outsiders. They are lost to this particular world, and the emotions running in the conversation. Some try half heartedly to make the odd comment with little impact, others don't even try. The consequence of working for the football bore, is that underperformance of 'insider' colleagues may be tolerated, because they are part of the banter, whilst high performers can underperform because they feel isolated from the 'in crowd'.

This is just one example of managing generically. If you treat all who work for you in exactly the same way, you are in effect in a 'command and control' mindset. You are using your position in the hierarchy to impose those things which matter to you, on others. The Asda way of working demanded that leaders got to know their people as individuals. If you know Mary hates football, you know not to talk about last night's game. You talk about her children and what they are doing when they go on holiday. If Jane loves Manchester United, you can wade in with some football banter.

How often do you hear of someone say "I treat my people how I would like to be treated"? It seems to be a good maxim. But it is absolutely wrong! The football bore will be able to carry on regardless, boring half his team rigid, if he treats people how he would like to be treated. Because he loves football, he assumes everyone will enjoy his enthusiastic commentary. The tougher maxim is this:

treat people how <u>they</u> would like to be treated. In order to do this, you have to find out what makes them tick, no matter who they are. This is something you do naturally with your boss. You know it makes sense to find out what he or she likes, what impresses, and most importantly what they don't like. I would suggest that the football bore never talks about the match last night if his boss doesn't like football... so why does he subject his team to it?

Asda charged all store managers with getting to know something about all their people... even when their store employed 500/600/700/800 colleagues (to treat people how they... would like to be treated). It is vital that you know that someone has 3 children under 5 years of age. That individual is going to have a few years of real logistical pressure balancing job and family. If you help at critical pressure points, you can and will build enormous loyalty. If someone else has a terminally ill relative, your empathy and support through that trauma will produce the same result. This is not just about being nice... it is the right thing to do on a human level, but it makes absolute commercial sense too. If you handle these issues badly, you will engender low morale, high absence, poor customer service and high labour turnover. As a consequence, your shop keeping (or whatever your business) will produce inconsistent results. Good leadership and a strong management skill set will produce the opposite... loyalty, soul and spirit on the job... and service / shop keeping outperformance.

Knowing about your people is not just about managing problems or issues outside the workplace either. Your people will be involved in many things outside their work.

Some will be parent governors; some will be running the local scouts; some will be musicians; some will have sporting credentials and some will be heavily involved in charitable work. The list is almost endless. The key is to tap into those talents, by getting to know your people. If you can bring the 'whole person' into the workplace, then you begin to harness the spirit, body and soul of the individual, rather that just their body. The Asda business did an incredible amount for charity over the years, both in terms of raising cash, and volunteering time and labour into community projects. That was because the business recognised that integrity with the community was good for trade, but also did this by tapping into the abilities, interests and passion of employees.

An example of Asda Magic in this context was Anne Marie, who was passionate about working for charity. Her store manager recognised this in the process of getting to know his people. He realised her abilities and drives were exceptional in this area. Not only was she good at her job, she exhibited exceptional ability in community and charitable work. Her talents were harnessed in the store as a consequence, and she did some amazing work raising money for good causes. Anne Marie became so effective, she was asked to help other local Asda stores, in the city in which she worked, with their charitable work and community links. Anne Marie was ultimately responsible for Asda winning awards from the City Council for charitable and community ventures. This all happened because the local manager recognised the power in the individual, and allowed it to flourish. Leaders have an awesome opportunity to see the potential of individuals.

There are many people like Anne-Marie in the Asda business, and I believe that they are in the workforces of every business. The difference is that Asda set out to get to know them; know their skills, aptitudes and interests. Asda gave them a channel to shine... and was simply amazed by the results. Asda harnessed those school governors, the captains of sporting teams and looked to use their skills in management! You will have some 'Anne Marie's' in your own businesses. The question to ask yourself is whether you are creating a style of management and behaviour that seeks to allow their talent to flourish?

Managers can nurture their people, or they can close them down. I talked earlier about listening to your people, and more importantly about responding. I quoted my example about the idea of shift swap emerging from listening to colleagues. That great idea, which has positively impacted the absence costs of the business, was almost killed at launch by management. Some of them thought it was more important to be 'in control' than to hand a piece of that control to their people.

In order to become a high performing organisation, I believe that you have to demand that your style of management operates in the way you want it to. The autocratic manager is becoming extinct as a viable model. Generations X and Y will not be effective if managed in that way, and society as a whole doesn't respond effectively to that model of leadership. The 'I'm in charge' command and control style is inept, and will 'switch off' the heart and soul of your people. It is a statement of the obvious, but people never actually leave companies. People leave their line manager. As I have already stated, if you have a turnover issue in your business, the intellectual response is frequently directed toward pay and remuneration levels. Every anonymous leavers survey I have ever conducted (and I have seen a few in my time) tells me that pay levels come somewhere between 5th and 7th on the list of leaver reasons. Somewhere near the top comes 'my manager's style', and the ability to 'flex' my hours around the demands of family.

When you conduct a face to face exit interview, the results are very different. People always tell you they are leaving for better pay in the new job. This is a complete 'red herring'. No one, in their right mind, ever began to look outside for a job which paid less. Even if it is pennies per hour, they go for something paying a little more. The real question to ask is, why did you start looking? If the line manager is the reason for looking, and they find you intimidating, or they just plain don't like you, they are hardly likely to broach the matter on leaving. They are more likely to tell you the real reason in an anonymous survey questionnaire. That will reveal that managers often cripple the company culture in the eyes of the employee. For the employee, their line manager is the company.

Asda made major progress on improving management style and leadership over time. This became obvious in the engagement survey results. As style began to change, so did the commercial results. The two things are inexorably linked. Many companies today are talking about triple bottom line accountability, and it is becoming accepted wisdom by world class businesses.

To give you an example of the power of such a change in management style, let me tell you about a colleague listening group in one of Asda's London stores a few years ago. I encountered a bit of Asda magic which came straight from the change in leadership and management style. Remember this was a London store. This was not some northern rural location. This was a store in the middle of an industrial / commercial estate with loads of alternative jobs in call centres and offices, all paying far better than the retail sector generally. I was listening to some colleagues talking to me about the store… I was asking them what it was like to work for Asda, and asking about the management team and the store manager in particular. One lady told me she had held numerous previous jobs in retail and in office work. Then she said something magical which has lived with me ever since… she said "David, I have worked for many companies; I am pretty well travelled and worldly wise, but because of the way I have been treated in this store, I will <u>never</u> leave".

'Never' is a significant word in this context. I was amazed to hear someone say they would never leave an hourly paid retail job, but she said it with forcible conviction. The group went on to tell me what a good management team they were working for, and how good their store manager was. It was 'music' to my ears. There is great pleasure in hearing 'from the troops' that your style aspirations as a business are delivering for them. Asda's retention with 18% labour turnover was the best in the food retail sector, and much better than a sector average of 40%. I heard about one competitor's store in another retail chain which had a target of 100% labour turnover! Clearly their actual turnover was worse than 100% per annum. A store with 100% labour turnover is in absolute crisis. Very low labour turnover is unhealthy, but heavy turnover is a massive cost to your business in re-hiring; induction costs and general loss of experience. It is debilitating to your business model. Asda, took pride in strong retention in a very tough competitive sector. Management style is a key factor in driving the culture in which people want to live and work. Productivity will only thrive in the right culture, and much of that 'atmosphere' is created through leadership and management style.

There is however, another point I want to make about management and leadership. That point is really about accountability and delivery. Managers and leaders… to whom much is given… much is expected from them in return. Asda worked to create a culture and style that welcomed new colleagues into the 'Asda family' and made them feel they could make a full and rounded contribution. At the same time, managers were also required to deliver with pace and accountability. The aim was for achieving world class performance. There is a real danger in driving engagement, that you can lose the focus on accountability. If managers slip into 'pacify and socialise' style, then performance will deteriorate. Driving for engagement is not an easy option. It's tough to get right. Leaders have to learn how to take their people with them. This is the key to accessing discretionary effort…….winning hearts and minds.

Perhaps the best illustration of my point comes from a story about Sam Walton… the founding father of the first Wal-Mart store in Bentonville Arkansas. Wal-Mart has gone on from that single store, to become the world's largest retailer. Sam Walton was famous for going into his stores around the U.S. and walking the shop floor. I have watched a lot of video footage of Sam Walton, wearing his baseball cap, kneeling down with a bunch of associates. His style was to listen to their issues and suggestions about their store. He wanted to pick up on what customers had said about the store and associate suggestions for change. In store, Sam Walton's style was very much like a 'benevolent uncle'. He recognised retail was hard work, and people were not on a massive wage. His purpose was to create a retail community to enable his people to give their best to customers. However, I have spoken with many who worked for him in a management capacity in the home office in Bentonville, and Sam's approach there had a subtle twist. One guy who talked to me said "within a month of having started in a middle management role, Sam invited me into his office". His approach was very direct. "Now then young man, I'm paying you a big salary, what have you done for the business so far, and what are you doing to deliver in the next 6 months?" He would make a note on his pad, and he would check up on what you said. If you want to fully understand what made Sam Walton tick as a leader, read his book 'Made in America', it's an insightful read about the growth of the world's largest retailer.

Leaders and managers have to be able to take and expect accountability… and the pressures that go with their reward levels. But, they must not 'kick down' as a means of 'sharing the pressure'. Great leaders enable performance and stretch their teams by switching on their wider capabilities. Poor leaders 'kick', which produces short term performance, fear and business upheaval. In the medium term, this model will not maximise performance… and the side effects on people are always corrosive. In the medium to long term, engagement levels will decline with a 'kick down' style, and so will business performance. The biggest indicator of incorrect style is high labour turnover, and management will always blame pay levels, rather than looking to themselves and their leadership.

Asda developed a leadership model to encapsulate this thinking, and describe the leadership philosophy in a very simple and understandable way. A means of communicating to thousands of managers in a way they could easily relate to. This was the leadership jigsaw.

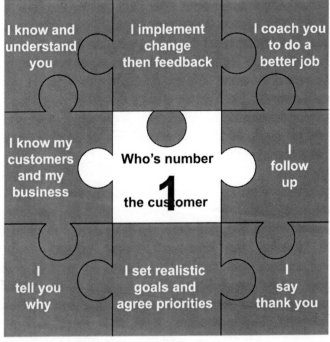

Diagram 5 – Leadership jigsaw

On the reverse side of the jigsaw was a mirror. This was to remind individual leaders to take time to know and understand themselves. Self awareness is a vital component for successful leadership, and the market proliferates with descriptive models. In essence, if you can understand what type of individual you are, and the effect you have on others, you will have a clearer insight into the effective management of people. It is essential that you play to your strengths, and talk to your team about mitigating your weaknesses. Great leaders always admit their weaknesses to others, and since those weaknesses are always known by others....it moves the leadership game to a new level. It builds trust.

One book that both the Asda business and myself found helpful was the Jim Collins book "Good to Great", which is one of those management books based upon facts and real companies, studied over long periods of time, in order to elucidate what works... rather than just 'guru' opinions. This book reminded leaders to look 'out of the window' when performance was good (i.e. recognise it is a joint effort in which all are involved), but to look 'in the mirror' when things were not going well and performance was poor. Underperformance is always a leadership issue... Asda leaders were given a mirror on the reverse side of the leadership jigsaw, for that very important insight.

The first piece of the Asda leadership jigsaw was about "knowing your people"

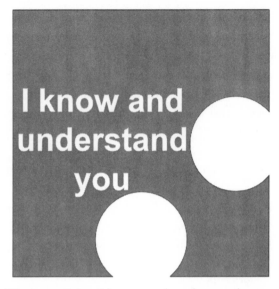

Diagram 5.1 – I know and understand you

Asda challenged managers to really get to know their people, to manage them differently, to tap into their potential. You can't get the best out of people if you don't know something about them. There isn't much more to say that I haven't already said on this point, except to say that great leaders excel in this aspect. I worked for a guy many years ago in my working life before Asda. He was exceptional at remembering names and facts about people. It was before the days when people wore name badges to help you with this sort of thing. He could remember who you were, what was happening in your life, and chat with you like a long lost friend. Yet, he was very senior, and people knew he didn't have to remember all that stuff about them. The effect of that behaviour by that senior leader was 'electrifying'. People thought he was fabulous. They would walk up vertical walls for him when he asked for something to be done. His gift was exceptional, but we all have the power to use some of that 'magic' with our people. Taking time out to personalise your style is time well invested.

Diagram 5.2 – I know my customers and my business

The second piece of the Asda leadership jigsaw was "I know my customers and my business". Being really good with your people, with a high level of self awareness, counts for very little if you aren't close to customers with an intimate knowledge of your business. We've all seen those hideous 'back to the floor' TV docusoaps where executives make complete fools of themselves going on the shop floor, and it's immediately obvious they are 'fish out of water'. At Asda, very little was said publicly about this, but managers just got on with it on a day to day basis.

Asda had a wonderful process every Christmas, whereby most of the people in Asda house, the head office, would go and work in the stores around the UK, to help the retail effort, at the time of the biggest 'spike' in sales. Many of those people were checkout trained; or they were adept at moving vast amounts of chilled food or beers/wines and spirits onto the shelves for customers. Working in stores on a regular basis was a great orientation into the practicalities of a retail business. It was a great finishing school. In my experience, the best businesses are run by leaders who are very close to what is going on at the grass roots level. Asda had regular and systematic processes for holding listening groups with customers; packing bags for customers at checkouts to elicit casual feedback about stores; and also 'accompanied shopping'... going around the store with a customer to understand what they thought, what they bought and what their observations were.

Customer research is fantastic for understanding customer behaviour, but nothing resonates for leaders quite like first hand knowledge. It was a piece of that Asda magic to devise means of being close to colleagues and customers on a personal level. I particularly remember one such accompanied shop with a lady who was a widow, living on a widow's pension, with three children aged between 6 and 11. She told me how much food three growing children consumed, and how hard she found it to make ends meet on a fixed income. I observed that she bought not one single 'brand' during her large food shop. All her selections were Asda's own label or economy brand. She also had a laser focus, picking and examining every product for their date codes. She wanted to ensure nothing went 'out of code' quickly at home to be wasted... she just couldn't afford it.

It's one thing to know 'intellectually' that Asda's customers demand value, and are likely to shop in a particular way. It's an entirely more vivid matter to experience that at first hand. I found it enervating to spend time with customers as well as to read the market research. It's good to know your business, and what your customers are thinking. I don't know how you can lead well and make the right decisions unless you are in touch in this way. I have had the privilege to serve alongside an executive board for many years who believed in this leadership principle. When your senior leadership colleagues know what customers are thinking; it makes many of the key business decisions much simpler, and more intuitive.

Diagram 5.3 – I set realistic goals and priorities

Following hard on the heels of knowing your customers and your business, is the leadership principle of 'setting clear goals and objectives.' Again, this sounds really simple and obvious. Yet how many examples can you think of, where businesses don't have goals which are clear and simple. Complexity is the enemy of delivery, and yet human beings seem unable to resist complexity. I'm a big subscriber to the KISS principle… 'keep it simple… stupid'. If you can resist complexity when all around you are building it in… you will be much more successful than them!

The other key principle in setting objectives is that they should all tie back to the headline objectives for the whole business, for the particular year in which plans are being made. In turn, they must tie into a 5 year horizon plan, which delivers the BHAG (big hairy audacious goals). This in turn should tie back to the mission/purpose and values.

Try this test on your own personal objective setting. How do you stack up to that simple aspiration of aligning every objective in a clear simple fashion? Part of the Asda magic was to constantly strive for simplicity. Simplicity and clarity of purpose leads to pace and motivation; these things are tied together. They cut down the frustrating and sapping bureaucracy which organisations tend to perpetuate. It is always a worthwhile investment for a top leadership team, to thrash out the simple big goals and objectives. If the top team doesn't provide clarity and simplicity… then everyone will operate in a divergent, confusing and demotivating fog.

Allan Leighton, Asda's chief executive in the late 1990's, often used to quote that "simplicity is divinity in business". He was right. Your job as a leader is to provide clarity in a world of complexity and confusion. If you do a few of the right things well as a business… you will be a winner. I hope you're beginning to get the hang of the simplicity of this leadership model from Asda. Here comes one of the most critical elements of the leadership jigsaw.

Diagram 5.4 – I tell you why

It really isn't enough to set clear objectives and goals, and expect people to get on with it. The human psyche has a real inbuilt desire to understand; to know what's going on behind the scenes. We are sentient and inquisitive beings. The reason we have always discovered new scientific principles; medical cures; or explored new places, is that we are essentially a pioneering race.

Work is exactly the same. Tell people clearly what to do, and you will get some output. Take time to clearly explain the context of the decision, and how the objective was set. Tell them what is going on behind the scenes. Tell people what is going wrong and what you are worried about. Make them feel involved and a part of the big picture, and effort blossoms into a whole new level. When your people feel 'in the loop', you begin to access their discretionary effort. It becomes their business as much as it is yours.

I talked about communication at some length in Chapter 6. This part of the jigsaw relies upon exactly the same thing.....communicate, communicate, communicate. As a reader, you will no doubt be thinking that it is common sense to communicate with your people. However, all my management experience tells me that 'common sense' is an oxymoron. It's actually 'rare sense' in reality, because so few people practice it in order to make it 'common'.

A few businesses issue clear instructions / mandates / policy statements. Many do not take the time and trouble to fully explain the context of what is happening, and get everyone on board. If you can embody 'I tell you why' in your belief system as a leader, you will run your business in a completely different way. You will also find your results sprinkled with a piece of Asda magic! It really does work.

Diagram 5.5 – I implement change then feedback

One of the principles Asda had to push hard when developing the leadership style of the business, was to get people to 'implement first, and then give feedback if they didn't agree.' This principle was necessary in Asda as a consequence of the whole engagement process. Asda found, over time, that people had become so used to challenging everything, that getting things done was becoming difficult at times. There is real power in involvement, but you don't want a business where single points of failure 'dent' your ability to implement major initiatives. As a consequence, Asda developed a 'suspension of doubt' principle, asking people to act first then give the feedback, if they didn't think the business had done the right thing, to avoid paralysis from too many critics and varied opinions. This also fitted well with the no holds barred culture.

I don't want to convey the picture that everything in the Asda cultural journey was 'plain sailing'. Like any business, Asda made mistakes. Mistakes are part of everyday management life, and can be positive, if the business learns from them. This leadership principle in the jigsaw was introduced as a piece of learning designed to plug a potential operational/performance weakness, arising from a highly engaged and questioning workforce.

Diagram 5.6 – I coach you to do a better job

One fundamental skill which all good leaders need to be able to deploy is coaching. Asda strongly emphasised the ability of leaders to be able to coach others, from the shop floor upwards. People have a need to be shown the 'tricks of the trade'. This should be at the elbow, one on one... spending quality time with people. A strong leader has to 'slow down' in order to coach.

I'm sure we have all worked with a leader who is like 'tigger'. These sort of leaders run around, frequently generating action, but causing general mayhem. It's exciting to be around them, but it's not good for excellent execution or delivery. By contrast, I'm sure we've worked with a few people who have taken the time and trouble to show us things or explain how something works. Taking 'time out' prevents recurring errors happening, ensuring people have 'got it', and will then also share their experience gained with others.

Those of us who have been parents often do this intuitively. We are constantly explaining to our inquisitive children how things work. We show, we explain, and if necessary we explain and show some more until they get it right! We are natural coaches as parents, and take some pride and delight in doing it. How come then, many leaders don't bring that innate skill into the workplace? Do we just believe they should know their stuff? Just because people are being paid to do a job, doesn't mean they wouldn't benefit from additional skills coached by their leadership.

Diagram 5.7 – I follow up

Having taken on board all the leadership skills described so far in the jigsaw model, surely all will be well with performance? Sadly this is not so. It is a fact that many of the people who work with you, will need to know that you always follow up.

Asda used a simple maxim for this principle 'DWYSYWD', that is 'do what you say you will do'. If you set some objectives/goals for delivery, your people need to know that you are serious, and that you will be coming back around to check. There is a real sense in which those things that get measured get delivered.

Some leaders are 'initiative junkies'. I suppose Belbin would define them as 'plants'. They are great at starting things off... full of enthusiasm. But, they are quickly bored with delivery of the day to day work, and they are quickly off onto the next big challenge. If you lead in this way, your people will quickly realise they should only respond to the latest thing, and they take the cue to drop the matters you don't follow up on. If you don't follow up... people naturally think it is not important to deliver.

My personal system was to keep a day book. I had all my actions listed against specific people, and they knew I kept the book. I let people see me write things in it... this was all part of my own 'signalling' of intent. I was certainly not infallible, and though I had a pretty good memory, there was always so much going on, that I really relied on a system for 'keeping track'. I believe that if you follow up consistently, people will see you as a good leader, not as a 'nitpicker'. It shows you care and what they are doing is important to you. It will also improve the performance of your business!

Diagram 5.8 – I say thank you

Finally, the last principle of the Asda leadership jigsaw was in itself a piece of 'Asda magic' (which has a whole chapter dedicated to it later – see principle six). Suffice to say at this stage that reinforcement is a powerful principle, and thanking people....... another piece of 'common sense'. It is 'rare sense' because so many managers forget to do it. Asda turned saying 'thank you' into an art form. I can't stress the importance saying thank you too much to readers of this book. More on this subject in chapter 10.

The leadership principles of the Asda business were always developing. Having used the leadership jigsaw for two years, and measured all managers against those principles in two consecutive leadership surveys, Asda took the learning, and moved the model on again. The aspiration of the Asda team was to lead a world class business, and raising the bar on leadership was a way of life. In order to become world class... Asda will need to become ever more adept and fleet of foot, in terms of leadership and style of management. Leadership is not a static dry theory, it is a living and breathing thing. Leaders must continue to expand and develop their skills, in a simple understandable way... it's a major part of what being a high performing business is all about.

Summary points – style of management and leadership

- Getting things done willingly and really well with and through others
- Energise your workforce... whether you use the term empowerment or engagement... it's about getting people on board
- Make sure people know they are doing 'worthwhile work' at all levels in the business
- People leave managers not businesses
- Develop an end to end leadership model and live by it

Your action notes – style of management and leadership

How would you define the style of management / leadership in your business?

What changes will you now make / what points have forcibly hit home?

So... what went wrong?
Style of management and leadership

Leadership style is probably the most difficult thing of all to get right. The 'tone and style' of leaders is such a complex subject. Asda wrestled more with leadership and changes to it than any other area of the culture. Changes to the model were not fundamental in methodology or beliefs, but 'tweaks to the tiller' to enable Asda to move on in high performance terms. I can't remember a single year during my 15 years in the Asda business, that we didn't amend or revise the appraisal process in some way. This is just the striving of the business to get better, rather than any major change of philosophy.

The fact remains, that people find leadership tricky and Asda was no exception to that rule. Leadership tends to work better when the business is performing. We can all probably achieve some 'cutting edge' things when the business is performing well. The real test comes when things are going wrong; controversy rages; people clash. There can be a whole myriad of highly charged issues. In the real world of frenetic business activity, it can never be all 'plain sailing'. In my experience, under real pressure, you always get some leaders who default to the wrong style. If this happens regularly, rather than a one off, the organisation has to firstly be aware, and secondly to deal with the issue. Asda developed mechanisms for detecting problems, and sometimes coaching could rectify the leadership issue. Sometimes people were just unable to manage and lead in the right way, thereby limiting their results. Those managers, in some cases, had to part company with the business.

This was part of the day to day activity of the organisation. Attitude and engagement surveys and 360 feedback on manager behaviour, together with listening groups, are the 'litmus paper' which indicates where leaders are delivering in appropriate or inappropriate ways. Dealing with managers who are 'outliers', and failing leaders became part of normal business life at Asda. Management behaviour was a recognised issue, which was not ignored. In some businesses, leadership underperformance and bad behaviour is routinely tolerated. This is the route to disaster, and the performance of all employees is dragged down as a result. I know of no business that gets this right all of the time. It's a constant battle, but one very much worthy of the fight.

CHAPTER 9

Principle 5 Remove your underperformers / push your talent

> "All the world's a stage, and all the men and women merely players; they have their exits and their entrances; and one man in his time plays many parts"
>
> William Shakespeare
>
> "Either back us or sack us."
>
> Jim Callaghan
>
> "Talent is cheaper than table salt. What separates the talented individual from the successful one, is a lot of hard work."
>
> Stephen King

I'm sure we've all read about Jack Welch at GE, whether that concerns him spending a claimed 50% of his time on people matters as a chief executive, or his remarkable period of success and growth at the helm of that business. The point I want to bring out about Jack Welch concerns his determination to remove the bottom 10% of his managers each year, in an effort to improve the performance of his business. I'm not saying this was right, but that his focus was interesting.

Performance matters. Building a high performance culture isn't always about positive actions. It is certainly about facing into your issues. If you don't do this, then you will be carrying 'passengers', and tolerating some 'organisational terrorists' who slipped into the ranks unobserved.

PepsiCo... another fast moving organisation, was famous for a period where executives were even more fixed on this point of removing underperformers. They had a period of time when they removed the bottom 20% of managers each year... a really tough 80/20, rather than GE's comparable 90/10. Interestingly, neither business still does this, but there was a period where they felt it necessary in order to move performance to a different level. I'm not in favour of defined numbers for percentage removal of managers, but I am firmly in favour of taking action regarding underperformance.

Despite having said that, management and leadership aren't just about the positives. It doesn't make removing people from the organisation an easy task. In an organisation like Asda, which had strong values and a real belief in building a strong culture, it was correspondingly tougher. If your organisation doesn't care very much about people, logic dictates it is easier to take action.

During a tough period for Asda in 2005, a number of redundancies were made. It was tough on everyone. But the business emerged stronger from that episode. Some people wrote to me to say "how could you allow this to happen?" I felt it very personally. In a sense, they were right. 'The Board of a Company is responsible for the success or failure of a business. I would like to have presided over 15 straight years of total success. But real life has a few bends and bumps in the road. Overall, Asda outperformed more often than not, and punched above its weight as a high performing business.

I believe that successful performance occurred because Asda faced into underperformance as a business. In my experience, most executives hate to face into underperformance. It is one of those tasks which appears to strike fear into the heart of the leader. In their excellent book 'First break all the rules', Marcus Buckingham and Curt Coffman talk about great managers being the ones able to terminate people, whilst at the same time keep the relationship alive. Some managers hire additional cover to hide underperformance; whilst others keep everyone at arms length, in case they have to remove one of the team. Great managers, however, employ 'tough love'. They strive for excellence in performance and don't tolerate 'average' for long. 'Love' in this context, is about respecting the person even when their talents don't fit. Buckingham and Coffman argue that 'manager assisted career suicide' is sometimes the answer. Truly great managers are able to do it well, and the individual can still think well of them.

People who are underperforming usually know it, and tend not to be happy in their role. They may be looking for the release to a less pressured situation, and for someone to take charge of the situation. After the trauma of removal, the individual will often be in a better place mentally, in a new role which better suits their skill set and talents. The trick is to handle the situation sensitively. This is never easy. I have seen some disastrous outcomes, but also some superbly 'sensitively handled' removals.

Sometimes the individual reaction is so negative, a disaster cannot be avoided. Often, the manager has a big influence on how the separation is handled. Did the manager 'flag' underperformance in good time, and handle the feedback well? Did they offer training, coaching and support genuinely? Did the manager indicate it wasn't working, and that a change would have to be made? Did the manager treat the individual with respect in order to preserve their personal dignity?

Asda leaders were encouraged to use tough love for a number of years; and it became part of the vocabulary of management. However, it is much easier to say than to do. It has to be said that if you do not deal with problem people... your bottom performers, then they will drag your performance backwards, and damage your own credibility with those who work for you. In the chapter on hiring for attitude, I talked about those you hire making a massive statement about your culture to employees inside the business. So do those individuals that you fire. Those two acts, hiring for attitude, and firing for underperformance hold the cultural 'balance' of your business. Any system has to be in balance. You need to be seen to act effectively on both issues to exhibit really effective leadership.

I like to illustrate this point via a 4 box model, to help put some logic around this issue:

	PROBLEM	STARS
High	Great performance bad behaviour (need to change style)	High performance great behavioural traits (push and promote)
	UNDERPERFORMERS	PROBLEM
Low	Poor delivery poor behaviour (remove from your business)	Don't deliver great personality fit (neet to deliver or won't be around)

(The Numbers) PERFORMANCE

Poor — BEHAVIOUR — Strong
(feedback via engagement survey results / 360 feedback)

Diagram 6 – 4 box on performance and behaviour

This matrix is a concerning one in some senses. Implicit here is that a fair proportion of your business could be delivering, but not in the right way through people. Equally concerning, is that you may have a fair proportion of lovely friendly people who fit culturally, but just aren't delivering their numbers. The aim in a high performance culture is to move the whole business towards the top right quadrant. High performance businesses want great delivery and a great style of leadership. The Asda Way of Working was about getting things done with and through others, willingly (great style and behaviour) and really well (great delivery). This recognises that peak performance only occurs when leader behaviour is truly appropriate.

Asda adopted a 10/80/10 approach to performance management and performance appraisal. Asda did not specify losing 10% of managers per annum like Jack Welch at GE, or 20% per annum like PepsiCo a few years ago. However, there was a forced ranking of manager performance to achieve a normal distribution curve of manager performance across the business.

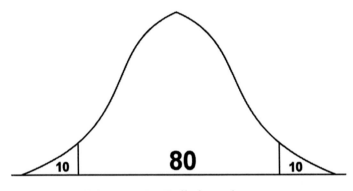

Diagram 7 – Bell shaped curve

In Asda, the bottom 10% were being worked on at all times via a programme called 'coaching for improvement'. The outcomes would either be a move to acceptable performance, or a parting of ways. Any business which aspires to high performance has to tackle performance management.

What do the Asda alumni have to say?

Allan Leighton
"Removal of underperformers is part of 'tough love'. It's very hard. Asda was a performance based culture. The culture was so strong that the business rejected people quite quickly if they didn't perform. People failed fast if they didn't fit."

Dave Cheesewright

"I learnt a lot about performance management in my time at Asda. I'm a great believer in the power of encouragement. But there has to be rigour in dealing with underperformance. The natural default if people don't deliver is to assume it is them. First eliminate the barriers of training or infrastructure. If you do let people go, you need to be sure you have looked in the mirror, and removed those barriers first."

Richard Baker

"It's a complete business necessity to remove underperformers. When times are tough, you find out who is and who is not good. You have to act early. The day they go, performance improves. If you don't deal with this, everyone else is demotivated. You won't become the best company to work for by being 'cuddly'. Tough love is what is required."

Paul Mason

"Having moved into the world of private equity and slimmed businesses, it is critical to take out 'double banking', and you have to be able to identify the people who haven't got the capability to change. Always change out the 'cynics' at the coffee machine first. It sends a signal to the others, and you have a chance to change the majority."

This is not easy material to write about, in what is essentially a book with lots of positive examples about engagement and motivation. However, all my experience tells me that you have to take decisive action in this area if you are to have a great business. So many chief executives I talk with tell me that this is their big weakness. It would be totally inappropriate to quote any real life examples, but Asda put a lot of effort into exhibiting 'tough love'. I am still in touch with leavers from the Asda business, who have made a new successful life in other occupations and businesses. Your leavers say a lot about your culture and who you are. Leave this area alone at the peril of your performance culture. Your people will see the 'cop out' and respect you less. Effort and engagement will decline as a result. The choice is yours.

> "There is no substitute for talent. Industry and virtues are of no avail."
> Aldous Huxley

The flip side to the performance management coin, is the development of your future stars. Asda was great at both praising and developing talent. As a business Asda pushed talent, and achieved 70% of all new managers promoted from the shop floor. I was constantly reminded of the success of this as I travelled extensively around the UK. So many of Asda's successful and capable managers started on the checkouts as 'temporary stop-gap' never intending to stay. They were 'bitten' by the retail career bug and not only remained with the business, but went into management roles. Asda had a 'stepping stones' process which aimed to pick people from the shop floor and equip them for their first line manager role. This stepping stones process was replicated at all levels up the organisational hierarchy.

Local managers were challenged at their own appraisal with having a number of people in development, in their areas of responsibility, at any one time. This became the feedstock for the future. Any business is only successful if it has seedcorn for future talent. It is important to give people the confidence that they can progress, and to enable them to do so. Moreover, truly great leaders take calculated risks on people. What do I mean by this? It is really simple. You spot talent, you nurture it, and you give people an opportunity slightly before they are ready, knowing that you can support the early stages of their development. People respond, in the main, to early opportunity. If you make a mistake, you can always put people back into their comfort zone ensuring you talk them through what's going on to keep them with you.

This cycle of spotting, nurturing and early promotion is the key to a vibrant and fast paced performance culture. I've seen people initially overwhelmed by new challenges, but if they are made of the 'right stuff', and well supported, they quickly come through, producing fabulous results... and also achieve the right behaviours with others working for them.

Asda was a melting pot of top talent over the years. Many of the successful leaders of UK retail came through the Asda 'academy'. I don't believe it is accidental that so many Asda people went on to run companies. There was a sense of growing talent, and of real capability growing in the Asda business.

To be a vibrant and successful business, you have to make way for talent to come through. I'm not sure that Asda processes were particularly sophisticated in this area, and indeed many of the talent management systems I see in businesses seem overly complex, and too sophisticated for the average human to grasp, let alone move through. Asda never used the complex, or the sophisticated. I believe it is much more important to promote early; take calculated risks, and support people to come through. If you hire the right people in the first place, you can trust them to do good things in the business. Performance management requires you to deal with underperformers quickly. If you don't do this, you wont have opportunity to bring your stars through. Everyone in your business knows who is underperforming. The stars are also well known. The business expects great leaders to do the right thing on both accounts.

I think many so called 'experts' put far too much pseudo science into what is basically a very simple premise. Hire great people; push your talent and take calculated risks on great people. You will have the odd failure, since life is never a straight line equation. No people strategy is ever flawless, because people are wonderfully unpredictable. That's what makes us human! However, doing the right thing about performance management will produce the right results over time. It is one of the cornerstones of high performance.

Summary points – remove your underperformers / push your talent

- Every team has an underperformer
- Face into performance management
- Recognise that executives tend to avoid conflict with people
- Coach improvement
- Take risks on stars and support them
- Lose your underperformers but do it well
- Everyone knows your stars and your problems – be seen to be proactive
- Identify top talent and give opportunity early
- Don't over complicate talent programmes

Your action notes – remove Your underperformers /
push your talent

What will you do differently?

So... what went wrong?
Removing underperformers / pushing your talent

In my experience, performance management is the leader's biggest minefield. Making a bad job of the exit of underperformers is all too easy. Making the wrong call on potential talent is often clouded by the subjective trap of 'liking' certain people... maybe because the manager sees something of themselves in them. My career experience has taught me that performance management is the leader's biggest challenge. Most chief executives I talk to, tell me that they are not good at performance management.

Asda made some major mistakes on handling underperformance. This is in no sense perjorative, since Asda wouldn't be a real business if this were not so. When things go wrong, it is important to learn whether it was a rogue individual who was reacting very badly, or whether the manager concerned handled things badly. These issues are often hard to arbitrate. I have found it useful to change the person handling the individual in such cases, but this can undermine confidence. There is no infallible rule book for this sort of thing, because the reactions of human beings are complex. You may get anger; tears; silence; aggression or a mixture of any of those, when tackling underperformance. Some people are submissive, but come back aggressively after consulting a lawyer, others are completely sanguine and mature. My bottom line here is that you never know what is going to happen, but I still hold to my premise that your leavers are part of your alumni, and you should handle them professionally, with the aim of preserving human dignity.

When you make the wrong calls on pushing your talent, it can be just as painful. As a business which moved people forward, Asda made its share of mistakes here also. The 'peter principle' is ever true, that people are often promoted to their level of incompetence. People are ambitious; business is fast moving and talent hungry. You are always going to make some mistakes. Leaders are all human. Promotion reviews need to be as objective as possible. I would urge all readers to spend a lot of time on this important issue. Every organisation will continue to make mistakes in this area in the future. The real objective is to 'rise above' those errors, because the overall objective of pushing talent early is so important in achieving a high performance culture.

Chapter 10

Principle 6 Recognition

> *"There is a great man, who makes every man feel small, but the really great man is the man who makes every man feel great."*
>
> G K Chesterton

Recognition is such a simple, yet amazingly powerful concept. Many businesses spend the majority of their 'motivational' effort on building elaborate remuneration frameworks, as if that is the most important mechanic in moving the business in the right direction. The 'industry' of preparing data for remuneration committees grows every year.

Don't get me wrong, I believe remuneration is important. People need income to pay their bills, and people need to be compensated appropriately for what they do. I have spent a fair amount of my own time looking at remuneration issues. The bottom line is that remuneration has to be around market rate for the role or jobs concerned. Remuneration is about being a player in the 'game' of business, it is not about motivating your people.

The real issue here is that so many people ignore the findings of Frederick Herzberg from way back in the

1950s. His view was that money is a 'hygiene factor', and often plays the role of demotivator. How many people ever tell you they have too much money? What you will always hear are 'gripes' about someone getting more than someone else. There will be moans and groans about outsiders coming in on higher rates than long serving insiders on the management team. "Where is the reward for loyalty?" is a regular comment in pay surveys. Any manager reading this book will have heard all these comments, and many more. "Why don't you pay me for my specialist skills?" "Why don't you pay me for my level of service?" On remuneration, you just cannot win.

We have all observed the corrosive effects of highly leveraged bonus schemes, through the global banking crisis. It has become increasingly clear that one of the factors in the financial crisis, was the over incentivisation of key executives encouraged to lend to individuals who could not afford to repay. Prudence was originally the watchword of the banking profession but you could argue that excessive incentivisation dulled that natural instinct, causing financial chaos which required governments to step in. Remuneration is a powerful, but potentially dangerous tool.

Recent research carried out by the Massacheusetts Institute of Technology argues that the only appropriate and effective use of incentives occurs in the context of simple mechanical 'piecework' type tasks. They carried out research on US students, and in a relatively poor economic environment in India. In both cases, the results were identical. Where the work involved complexity, thinking and teamwork (in other words most tasks in the workplace today), incentives were shown to be counter productive. This is food for thought for the average remuneration committee. Should the reader be interested in this research, which merely serves to prove Herzberg correct, then the work of Dan Pink summarises the findings.

Asda's mission was to be the lowest price/best value retailer. There was no room at all for wasting money. In a business with wafer thin margins, remuneration could never be better than market average, or Asda could not offer great value to customers. The opportunity for above average remuneration lies in the premium product markets, and the customer has to bear the cost.

How do you motivate and engage your people, when you are paying the majority very little more than the minimum wage? I believe the elements I have already described around great communication and listening, make a huge difference to the motivation of people. Having the right style of management and leadership (and removing these who underperform) is hugely engaging. People truly respond to the right leaders (and love it when you take ineffectual leaders away). People are also highly motivated by the possibility of development and promotion opportunities for the best performers. Living in a meritocracy is hugely motivational.

In addition to this, I have found that the icing on the engagement cake is that of effective recognition mechanics within the business. Asda could be said to have 'overdosed' on recognition, quite deliberately. Recognition was a vital part of the Asda magic, and a cornerstone of the culture.

> "People ask you for criticism, but they only want praise."
>
> W Somerset Maugham

I had an amazing experience some years ago, which emphasised this point about the importance of recognition to me. I was in a listening group in one of Asda's London stores with about 15 colleagues. The store was old, and in need of some considerable capital spend to modernise and refurbish the store. There were all kinds of things they told me about the building, which made life hard work in that store. They told me all those issues, in detail, using graphic description and language. Asda had created a culture where people felt they could speak the truth without any fear of reprisal. They just told it like it was. That feedback is the 'breakfast of champions'(you need to hear it), but sometimes it just overwhelms you. I have sometimes sat listening to colleagues wondering where to start working on such honest feedback.

On this occasion, at the end of their tirade about the physical state of the store and the quality of leadership there, I asked the group if there was one thing I could fix and only one... what would the one thing be? My rationale was that you couldn't fix everything they had raised in one go, but I wanted them to specify what really mattered. What was their number 1 request for change? I had an expectation in my mind of the most important thing they might say (I was expecting them to ask for more money), but that was not what they said. Their number one request was, "just ask the management team here to say "thank you" for all the hard work we do, in a difficult environment in this store." I was blown away by their comment. Most of the things they had talked about would have cost £millions of capital expenditure to fix, and a major store renewal scheme. Their primary request was a 'thank you', which costs nothing. I learnt a powerful lesson that day. Saying 'thank you' looms large in the minds of those at work, and recognition matters hugely to people. People want to be recognised for what they do on a day to day basis.

The whole essence of what I am trying to describe for you is summed up in a statement from an Asda colleague in a listening group I attended in a store in Scotland. "This is the best place I've ever worked for praise and appreciation. It makes you feel good when you have worked hard and it is appreciated". I still have a strong sense that Asda had not done enough in this area, despite all the talking about it, the encouraging of leaders to do it, and the plethora of schemes we had for it. What I do know for certain, is that those who do use recognition well, have seen the power of it.

Asda 'overdosed' on recognition, as I have said. This began with some really 'zany' ideas in the early days. When I arrived in Asda, there was a scheme in operation to recognise those good at selling in the stores. The business was on its knees, and there was a real need to get a 'buzz' around selling product. In the early days of the Asda turnaround, a number of board directors had left the business, and their company Jaguar XJs were left behind but still on lease. Such staus symbols were no part of the leadership regime going forward, and the idea came about that they could be loaned for a month, to the colleague from the shop floor who sold the most of a sponsored product during the previous month. The scheme was branded the volume producing item, and colleagues were briefed about what their prize would be for sales uplifts. Colleagues jumped out of little old Ford Fiesta's into V6 Jaguars for a month, and they loved it. It has to be said that they also 'crashed and bashed' them a fair bit, but the motivational effect was spectacular. The cars only lasted to the end of their lease, but it was a fabulous recognition scheme, which illustrated the power of recognising great performance. Asda has since used mini convertibles along the same lines, but nothing worked better than those redundant Jaguars in the early days of the Asda turnaround.

Another idea from the early 1990s was the 'golden cone' parking spaces in the Asda house car park in Leeds. Like any large business based in a city, car parking was at a premium. Leeds is Asda's head office, and there were more people employed than the 750 car parking spaces available. In the original traditional hierarchical Asda culture, the spaces right outside the front doors of the offices were allocated to the chairman; chief executive; finance director and so on. The culture change swept away allocated spaces, and all spaces were on a 'first come first served' basis. The Asda chief executive and the executive board had no allocated parking. Those spaces outside the front doors became allocated to the 'golden cone' scheme, reserved for anyone nominated by the stores for offering great service. It became a great privilege to have a space reserved outside the front door, which recognised that you had given great service to the stores. It was even more important to send a signal to everyone working in Asda house that serving stores, who in turn served customers, was a vital task. The people who parked in those spaces outside the front door did so with pride. It was a fantastic recognition tool, which cost nothing, but became hugely symbolic.

One of the recognition traditions of Asda, before the early 1990's turnaround, was a thing called 'the silver club'. This was a lunch, held in the boardroom at Asda house in Leeds. The room was cleared of its board table, and small circular tables were installed for all those individuals achieving 25 years or more service. It was a little old fashioned, but an important celebration for those participating. As the company grew, so did the length of service of those in the business. When I joined Asda, 100 people attended the Silver Club, but those numbers of longs servers grew rapidly to thousands. Asda had the best retention in UK retail, and consequently had to quickly adjust attendance at this event to include only those colleagues achieving significant length of service anniversaries (25/30/35/40/45 years in the business). The big anniversary, as it became known, was part of the magic of Asda. The chief executive always attended, and celebrated long service recognition in some style. Attendees heard about 'what was happening in the world in the year you joined the business', and people were made to feel special. I loved that particular day in Asda, and so did the executives who attended to 'host' the tables. It's a big deal when someone has worked for your business for a quarter of a century, and even more so when their service amounts to 40 or 45 years. Recognition of loyalty may be an old idea, but it still has real meaning for people. I was talking to a colleague from one of the Leeds stores about a week after the big Asda anniversary. "What a fantastic event" she said. "That's what working for this company is all about. They really care." Recognition matters to people. It's not trivial. My contention is that recognition is worth much, much more than money. As a leader, you are showing people that you care about what they do on a day to day basis. In an age when loyalty is not common, celebrating loyalty to your business is massively significant.

Another big set piece recognition event at Asda was the 'Oscars' complete with arrival by stretched limo; a red carpet; and a glittering 'black tie' evening. Nominees watched a video profile of their great service deeds, and the whole thing had the suspense of the nominee envelopes being opened for the winners (just like the 'real' Oscars in the film industry). Ordinary people who had done extraordinary things in the business, got to feel recognised as stars of the business.

Let me bring the Oscars recognition scenario to life for you, by talking through a couple of stories. One of the Oscars stars worked as a porter in a store in Nottingham. He worked with a team of colleagues, and was a great friend to them all. You would want this guy on your team, he was a great worker. He had found that one of his team mates was unable to read. He coached him, and enabled him to be brave enough to deal with the problem. When I told his story at the Oscars ceremony, there wasn't a dry eye in house. Speaking of eyes, another star was an optometrist. He gave an eye test to a young girl who had been experiencing severe headaches. Her mother had previously taken her daughter to the doctor, who prescribed pain killers. The headaches did not go away, so she took her to accident and emergency at the local hospital. The doctors in the hospital said there was no detectable problem. This young optometrist looked in her eye and spotted an abnormality. It was the first slight sign of a brain tumour. The girl was rushed to hospital and they operated immediately. He had caught the problem and saved both her sight, and also potentially her life. You can imagine the applause at the Oscars when this young colleague was on stage being recognised.

It is also worth highlighting that fact that the whole Asda board attended. Each table was hosted by a director of the business. One guy seated next to me worked in one of Asda's Swindon stores. He said something to me which still 'haunts' me to this day. He said "in what other world would I get to sit with someone like you?" He was implying he was honoured to be sat next to a board director. I hadn't even thought about it. As leaders we often forget the potential effect we are having on others. They are delighted to be sat with significant people from their world of work. This kind of recognition matters.

The sequel to the story of the Oscar nominee from Nottingham came three years after the ceremony. I was walking from my car in a very full Asda store car park, on my way to a meeting, thinking about the content of what I was going to say. Suddenly a voice shouted

"David!" at the top of his voice. It was the Oscar winner from three years previously. This guy was a middle aged scotsman, not taken to suffering fools gladly I suspect. He literally ran across the car park, shook my hand until it nearly fell off, and told me that Oscars night had been the 'best night' of his life. That's a piece of Asda magic. Recognition matters to people. I've watched them on so many occasions being recognised, and they are visibly moved and proud. That is a moment of recognition which causes them to stretch for more. It encourages them, and raises morale generally because it encourages others to try harder to gain such recognition. It certainly breeds loyalty, and taps into the soul of the individual. Recognition is something which helps leaders to access the discretionary effort from individuals, which cannot be gained by barking orders, nor by money.

Lets hear what the Asda alumni have to say...

Allan Leighton
"This is the most powerful organisation I have ever seen."

Richard Baker
"What is good about Asda is that it has continued to innovate. Asda has been very strong around ways to engage colleagues and recognise their contribution."

Paul Mason
"The majority come to work to do a good job. It isn't just achievement, but recognising effort. We used

---

some Asda recognition techniques in Somerfield and I got both positive reaction and traction. You have to pay a fair wage, but recognise people alongside this. At Asda, you celebrated achievement."

Dave Cheesewright
"Recognition is massively important as a principle. All the research here in Canada tells me that not being thanked is the biggest cause for lack of engagement. Recognition doesn't cost much, but is massively important. We have instituted a scheme in the Wal-Mart stores in Canada called 'find 5 a day to recognise'."

Archie Norman
"People need to feel they have won in life."

Recognition drives performance by increasing the motivation of individuals and teams. Asda developed a plethora of schemes, to recognise high performance. However, a simple appropriate 'thank you' from your boss is probably the most powerful recognition of all.

My final story under this topic of recognition comes from Elgin in the far north of Scotland. Two Australian customers came into the Asda store in Elgin looking for two bottles of an unusual brand of single malt whisky. The store did not stock or sell that particular brand. The colleague serving them took their details to make enquiries as to whether the whisky was stocked elsewhere in any larger Asda stores carrying a different range, but to no avail. Not to be beaten, the colleague from the store went out and purchased those two bottles of single malt direct from the distillery. Meantime the customers went back to Sydney in their native Australia. But it is the next bit of the story which is incredible. One of the colleagues in store was visiting relatives in Sydney, and agreed to take the malt whisky out to Australia. She made contact with the customers, and delivered the whisky to their home. I can't imagine how amazed they were with that outstanding display of service. That really is service to the customer which is above and beyond the call of duty... and with a very international flavour to it. My learning principle here is that once people feel recognised for their contribution, they begin to do outstanding things as a consequence.

The maxim is that we should never underestimate the power of saying 'thank you'. People who live in an environment which recognises their effort will go to extraordinary lengths to give legendary service. When you see a good job done... recognise it... even if it is a simple personal 'thank you'. What you say really does make a difference to the performance of the receiver.

Summary points – recognition

- People want to be thanked
- Recognition is more significant than remuneration
- Remuneration is often a demotivator
- Overdose on ways to make recognition happen
- Force managers to be precise, not vague, with their praise
- Devise recognition mechanics which suit your business
- Involve your managers – make sure they know it's important
- Involve your customers – they are the unique judges of whether service truly was above and beyond the call of duty

Your action notes – recognition

What will you do to harness the power of recognition?

So... what went wrong?
Recognition

Despite all that Asda did in the area of recognition, and there was a plethora of action, there was still the feedback from colleagues in the business that their management team didn't say thank you enough. Over time, I heard this less frequently, but I still came across it. How do you instil the discipline of thanking people regularly as a mindset? I suppose this comes back to remembering the basics in a busy environment. It's common sense. But as we all know, common sense is not always common.

Let me illustrate how things can feel when a store was not being well led, and effort was not being put into recognising performance. These are extracts from some notes I took in a listening group in a London store in 2008:-

- "the managers don't say thank you."
- "some managers object when you are pulled off your department for queue busting."
- "teamwork needs to improve in this store."
- "there should be more social events, fun and buzz in the store."
- "we need more people developed to take control of parts of the store."

When I heard these comments, you can imagine I was not best pleased that those shop floor colleagues were being let down by their leaders in that location. Even after years of progress in improving a culture, you can get 'organisational terrorists' in parts of the business. I was very pleased that colleagues could articulate exactly what they should be getting from their leaders, and that enabled that store to fix what needed fixing.

With Asda's formal recognition schemes, there were always some stores that did not do this well, whilst others were absolutely diligent and brilliant. We're back to the human ability to implement, and the need to keep refreshing materials/content of schemes, in order to keep the principle alive. Recognition as a 'way of working' is hard work... but the prize of high engagement driving discretionary effort/service outperformance is worth striving for. I suppose it's a little like painting the Forth railway bridge; you can never stop.

CHAPTER 11

Principle 7 Creating "the buzz" / fun and a sense of community

> "Work is much more fun than fun"
>> Sir Noel Coward
>
> "Most people get a fair amount of fun out of their lives, but on balance life is suffering, and only the young or very foolish imagine otherwise."
>> George Orwell

I have long believed that most people come to work wanting to do a good job. Often it is bad management which can be the major obstacle to this happening.

Asda worked very hard to create a culture where 'work made fun gets done'. This is easier said that done in a retail business. In one sense, retail is very exciting; fast paced and ever changing. Seasons drive new ranges and new products. So, in one sense retail is the ideal place to create a sense of 'fun' around that level of pace and change. However, on the other hand, retail work is hard work, a seven day per week trading business, and in many cases 24 hours per day. Products are physically heavy to move around from delivery lorry to warehouse and on to shop floor shelf.

Just as an aside to illustrate the 'hard work' point, I remember talking to one Asda colleague in store. She was delighted by her job on the grocery department night shift. I asked her why, and she proudly announced "Since starting this job, I've lost over 30 pounds in weight. I've given up my gym membership, since there's no need to pay the annual fee. My job is my workout." That is both an example of how physically demanding retail work can be, but also how that particular colleague had the right mental attitude. For her, work was a workout. She was making her work fun!

For many Asda colleagues, it was the team entity which was their source of fun and engagement. They enjoyed the colleagues they worked with. Because they had been hired for a gregarious attitude, they became part of a vibrant culture, and worked well together. A team which works together regularly, can form a bond, and this can become 'fun'. There is often a healthy 'banter' which takes place in teams, and that fun/buzz enhances the productivity of the unit. The real challenge is to give individuals and teams the permission to have fun, and enjoy their work.

Sometimes businesses get this very wrong. There may be the odd manager who slipped the net on Asda's recruitment process. We all make hiring mistakes! These sort of individuals quickly became apparent because of the feedback mechanics the business had in place. In these circumstances, Asda changed the behaviour of these managers through coaching, or changed the manager via a parting of the ways. Every business has to deal with its leadership issues. Great managers enhance the culture, they are fun to work with. Poor managers constantly demotivate and drag performance in a downward spiral.

More often than not, Asda made the right hiring decisions. 93% of the people in the business loved working for Asda. It was a remarkable score for such a large retail business. One of the Asda colleagues from Lancashire loved her work so much that she travelled from her 'retirement home' in Spain, to work a couple of shifts each week with her work mates in her local Asda. That is remarkable dedication to her old work team, and a remarkable tribute to the magic of the Asda culture.

Quote from Steve McDermott business speaker & guru

"Asda are one of my favourite clients. Many years ago, I did a speaking engagement for them at Asda house (their office in Leeds). Now, have you ever had a thing where you visit somewhere for the first time and there is a buzz in the building? (And I'm not talking about faulty fluorescent lights) There's just something about the place and the people that make it feel special. Well, every time I visit Asda, it's always like that. So after the very first visit, I wanted to work with them. I wasn't sure why, apart from the people and the buzz." If you want to read more of Steve's impressions, they are in his book 'How to be a complete and utter failure in life, work and everything'. The Asda comments are on Pages 171 to 174.

One Asda people manager in a Manchester store gave an eloquent summary of 'the buzz' in the business. "I've been in the Asda business 22 years, and never intended to stay. Asda is the kind of place that develops you. Retail is very hard work indeed, but it's fun. There is a buzz to it. Asda has created something you want to be part of. If that wasn't the case, I wouldn't have stayed for 22 years!"

Some days, when a few things have gone wrong in your working day, and you feel that the business is not where it needs to be (we all know the foibles and weaknesses of our businesses... and often we 'get used to' all the good points so that we no longer see them) I found it a tonic to interview an external candidate. External interviewees who came into Asda house in Leeds all talked about the buzz of the place as they entered the atrium of the building. They described the place as having 'energy'; or a 'happening' sort of place. Asda house was a noisy building, with lots of activity and the 'hustle/bustle' you would expect from a fast moving retailer. There was no place for the hushed and often sepulchral reception spaces you find in some companies.

Quote from business guru Rene Carayol
Lets hear another story from another guru about the 'buzz' found at Asda. Rene Carayol is the author of 'Corporate voodoo' with David Firth. He is a broadcaster and guru who specialises in leadership, and often makes controversial statements in order to stir up debate. He had said something reported in the press, which was pretty derogatory about Wal-Mart, and his concern that they would 'spoil' Asda in the UK. So I invited him to come and visit Asda. Now I had no idea that Rene was an 'office

---

reception detective.' His tactic was to arrive very
early for his appointment, and to sit around and
'soak up' the atmosphere, in any head office he
visited. It told him an awful lot about the culture of
the business he was visiting. Rene thought the Asda
receptionists were very personable, and the atrium
of the building was a 'happening' sort of place. He
asked one of my team what they thought about
Asda, and received a eulogy of what a fabulous
place it was to work. He was bowled over by the
fact that I came down to reception personally
to meet him. I also took Rene to the 'late lunch',
which was a business update meeting for the whole
building; with a current music group playing guitar
and singing their latest single; a full financial update
for the month's performance; and some recognition
on stage for key individuals. Rene still uses the story
of his visit to illustrate the 'buzz' of a strong culture.
You can't manufacture these things. People can tell
a lot from the 'smell of the place', and I'm not
referring to your brand of cleaning fluid!!

I heard very similar comments to Rene over the years
of interviewing candidates. It was my own way of
measuring that the business was continuing to
demonstrate 'the buzz' to others, and exhibit its energy.
I trust that 'buzz' and sense of fun will continue for many
years to come in the Asda culture. It is a key component
of high performance. Creating a fun environment can
have a variety of elements. The Asda leadership had no
offices in Asda house. Not even the chief executive had
an office. The store managers didn't have an office either.

Accessibility matters to people. It changes the way a place feels. Those office complexes with every executive shielded by an outer office, and some assistant trained to 'repel boarders', say that you don't want to listen.

Asda leadership strove hard over the years to take work seriously, but not take themselves seriously. High performance is a real tangible objective, but is best achieved in a 'fun' way. People in Asda loved to see their chief executive and executive team leading visibly, but they also enjoyed them being 'gunged' in a gunk tank, or doing something suitably 'tough' as a challenge for charity. There is something good about a leader who can participate in the humour for 'children in need'.

Asda had a real desire to have fun. It was part of the Asda magic. As I visited stores, so many had pictures on the corridor walls in the areas at the back of house, where that 'work made fun gets done' mindset was replicated. With events in seasons, Asda people seemed to go to town on dressing up for customers, and also did the same thing with each other during social events evenings.

Alumni remarks – lets hear what they have to say about 'fun and buzz'…

Richard Baker
"Fun was regarded as OK behaviour in Asda. Nothing was perfect, but you were encouraged to push fast, and do a lot of things to create momentum. That was the buzz."

Tony de Nunzio
"Asda was about an absolute focus on people, which translated into high energy and motivation... and ultimately produced real customer focus."

Dave Cheesewright
"Above all, it was the people at Asda who created the 'buzz' and the fun element. Asda was competitive, and used humour, irreverence and informality, without losing the reality that business has to deliver. It's a rare thing, but it is that 'can do' informal environment which is so powerful. The culture of Asda had a humility. No one minded making a fool of themselves at Asda, which made it good fun. The caring nature of the business was infectious."

Allan Leighton
"I think fun is really important in organisations to keep the stress down... it increases the capacity to get more work done. At Asda, it made people feel good about doing things. A lot of the elements were very professional, but zany. That's what works!"

Paul Mason
"Fun attitude is a common thread amongst people who have worked at Asda. This includes self depracation. Never take yourself too seriously."

Justin King
"I have always thought business should be fun. Business takes itself too seriously. You need to have a smile. There was always a business meaning to the fun in Asda."

The other aspect connected with work being made fun, is work which involves the local community. There is a strong sense in which a retail business such as Asda needed to get involved with the local community. The community is built up of a myriad of customers. Customers are the people Asda was trying to serve, and working in the local community was part of a virtuous circle of 'putting something back', producing loyalty to the brand.

But, I believe there is more to it than that. People enjoy that sense of doing something for others. It feels like the 'right thing to do', it's an ethical issue. It's more than just the obvious commercial driver. I believe this was another piece of Asda 'magic'! You may be reading this, feeling somewhat cynical. "Lots of businesses do this sort of thing don't they, it mostly just gets in the way?" I hear you saying. That view massively underplays the potential of linking the community to the high performance potential of the business.

Let me tell you about an Asda colleague in order to illustrate the 'magic' of Asda people in their community. I want to talk to you about Jackie, who worked in an Asda store on the south coast of England. Jackie worked for the business for 27 years. She was a fabulous Asda colleague in every respect. Hard working; positive; a real role model. She didn't have a perfect life. Her husband was disabled, and she was the prime carer. She also had a disabled daughter. You would never know these facts. This lady was permanently cheerful. She loved her role in Asda. Always speaking on the mobile microphone in the store, selling to customers. She helped the store win many promotional events. She was really good at her job, and customers loved her friendly warm style. Colleagues who worked with her in store felt that way too. She became a bit of an 'agony aunt' to whom other colleagues would turn. If you had a problem, Jackie was the shoulder you would lean on. I guess, as you read this, you are more than moderately impressed that a lady with personal family pressures could achieve so much. "But there are many people like this" I hear you say. Let me go on to describe the 'magic' that was Jackie's work in the community. Jackie had a real concern about local kids who were drink or drug dependent, and she did loads of charitable fund raising work in that area. Through that work, she became a well known character with the local police (for all the right reasons!!) and worked tirelessly to generate cash for the local police officers to be able to use mountain bikes to patrol their local beat. She also generated a lot of cash, through the customers in store to help funding of the local air ambulance.

As if all this was not enough, Jackie had a soft spot for the local women's refuge. She could often be found there on a Sunday afternoon helping to cook them lunch. Despite her own problems at home, she even went to cook lunch there on Christmas day! Are you beginning to feel the 'magic' that this lady represents? Jackie saw a programme on television about autistic orphans in Romania. She was soon organising charitable work in store, and the community, and even went out to Romania, in her own time and at her own expense, to deliver aid to this particular orphanage. This wasn't a nice place with pretty children. This was a place where abandoned autistic children, whom nobody wanted, were living in squalid conditions. Jackie came back wanting to work even harder to help. She did more fundraising work, and made three further visits to Romania, which eventually resulted in an extension being built on the orphanage, with decent showers and facilities. What a remarkable force for good this lady has been.

I was thinking about how Asda might recognise Jackie. What possible recognition might be appropriate to her? In the end, I thought that because she had used her own holiday time to go out to Romania, Asda might give her an additional week's paid leave to relax. What did I later find that Jackie was proposing to do with that additional leave? She took that week to go back out to Romania. I get frustrated that the new year's honours list is awarding knighthoods and honours to the already rich and famous. As a nation, we should be recognising people like Jackie. Can you imagine the enhancement to the Asda brand that Jackie achieved in her community? This kind of thing is ethical, it's the right thing to do, to allow your people to follow their concerns about working for situations that matter through their place of work.

Creating an environment where people realise it is legitimate to have fun is vitally important.

At Google, each employee has 10% of their time to do anything they like, whether it is playing table football or whatever. They know creativity will thrive due to that freedom. Close it down, and you cramp innovation.

What do you do in your environment to make you workplace fun? Work made fun really enhances productivity. If you have a customer facing environment, even more so. Colleagues enjoyed the retail theatre of dressing up, and so did the customers. If relieves tension... it makes the day lift. Why do parents enjoy Disney when they know it's real people dressed in character suits? It's because it's a bit of fun.

Involvement in the community is even more powerful. It's the right thing to do, but it grips both your people and your customers alike. Despite the constant barrage of negative news we read and hear every day, there are armies of ordinary people out there who actually want to make the world a better place.

Summary points – creating fun / buzz / community and performance

- Work made fun gets done
- Create teamwork
- Aim for a buzz / energy in the workplace
- Get real involvement in your local community – it's ethical/the right thing to do
- Prepare to be surprised by what your people can / will do

Your action notes – how will you create more of a sense of fun/buzz/community in your business?

So what went wrong?

As far as the final principle of creating fun/buzz and a sense of community in the business, it is easily lost when leaders don't do what is right. So many of the principles of high performance are inter connected. Culture is a 'house of cards', and failure on one of the elements can cause things to come crashing down.

At times of cost pressure, Asda was guilty at times, of doing things which suppressed the fun. The remedy was to make cost saving part of the fun itself. You can make light of most things as a leader, if you really try. Those who have worked with me over the years will have seen me use the power of humour in difficult situations. It can be a great release, and a diffuser of tension. There are two mindsets to face cost cutting – getting on with it and getting under it. It is far better to play a 'winner tape' in your head than to play a 'loser tape'. The consequences of the two styles are very different.

Leaders need the objective in mind of keeping energy levels high, and not sapping people. If people can be allowed to be themselves and fulfil their potential, the business can pull through very difficult circumstances, and errors made by a minority of leaders.

CHAPTER 12

What's the evidence of Asda's success – a high performance culture?

"Nothing succeeds like success."

Proverbs

"If at first you don't succeed, try, try again."

William Edward Hickson

"For success, attitude is equally as important a ability."

Harry F Banks

"No matter what others do; do it better than yourself, beat you own record from day to day, and you are a success."

William J. H. Boetcker

"Faith in your own powers and confidence in your individual methods are essential to success."

Roderick Stevens

I have introduced seven principles, but what evidence do I have of Asda's success in building a high performance culture? Is my approach one of evidence based people strategy? Asda acquired a lot of glassware and metalware in the shape of awards for achievement and innovation in the people sphere. Many of those awards were for innovation in such things as flexible working practices; innovation in recruitment & selection processes; for a fabulous resourcing website and clever things around communicating employee benefits and share schemes.

Those awards were recognition within the field of human resources (or people in my preferred terminology), and were great things to win. They gave pride to a team of people who worked hard in their specialism to make Asda a great place to work. They certainly mattered, and I don't want to diminish them. I was particularly pleased when Asda was recognised for innovation in people by the CBI and named as 'the people's champion'. I appreciated that award very much indeed.

However, and there is always a but, these awards were made by panels of the 'good and the great', and do not take into account what the 'troops' of a company think. Many awards are an 'outside in' perspective by judges who assess projects submitted to them. My own view is that there is a lot more power in a survey result, when the employees of organisations themselves get to vote. Then it is not a matter of what was presented to a panel, who can be 'fooled' by a slick presentation, but the reality of what is really happening in a business at the grass roots.

I started this book by posing the question "how come an organisation of Asda's huge size, paying not a lot above minimum wage, could actually spend 5 years in the Sunday Times top 50 best places to work, and win outright as the number one best place to work in 2002?"

It is a remarkable achievement, when the methodology was not a judging panel of the 'great and the good' assessing companies, but the employees of the participating organisations returning attitude surveys about their own place of work. It amazes me that John Lewis; Boots; Marks & Spencer; Tesco and J Sainsbury have never got into the Top 100, and Asda was by far and away the largest entrant (the next largest being Nationwide building society at 15,000 employees).

However, even though Asda was immensely proud to be named the best place to work in the UK. Even though Asda maintained a top 50 placing for 5 years consistently, and became a laureate company of best places to work. Even though Asda was similarly recognised by the Financial Times and Fortune Europe magazine (alongside Ferrari in Italy – I loved that one!). I prefer the internal metrics. Internal metrics for me, have the ultimate importance. They are the foundation of business action and traction.

For me, the metrics which count in evidence based HR, are the internal ones. Asda ceased to enter the Sunday Times survey, because, in the end, it was distracting the business from its own internal listening process and follow up.

In 2008, the Work Foundation and the Institute for Employment Studies tested a range of people management practices with 3,000 employees, in order to assess their impact on organisational performance. The survey found that good people practices around engagement and development produced higher profit margins in businesses.

My own view, very strongly held, is that what a business does around engagement and motivating people does make a difference to the commercial success of the business.

If I go back to some data, from 1998, on the performance of the people key result areas, the Asda business morale index was at 70%; labour turnover was 27.94% and absence was 4%. Asda ended 2008 with a morale index of 92%; labour turnover of 18% (against an industry average of 40%) and absence at 3.2%. Those are real 'in house' solid measures of performance. To me, this is the real illustration that the culture of Asda moved forward, over a decade, and was a component part of improving business performance.

The question this then poses, rather than the generality of improvement, is whether a direct link to profitability can be established. Gallup, who are a world leader in examining this sort of data, put all the Asda stores commercial results, together with Asda 'we're listening' survey scores; customer service data; and perception data into their analysis process. They came back with some very interesting results. Not surprisingly, Gallup found a strong positive correlation between individual stores with a high 'we're listening' (morale and engagement) score and strong sales/profitability. I was able to establish a 'sweet spot' for morale, above which profits rose exponentially. The conclusion being that the stronger the culture, the happier your people are, then the more profitable your business will be. It makes absolute sense. I wonder why so many businesses underplay this vital component?

You may have read this book thinking "It's a pretty good story." You may have read this book thinking "It's all too good to be true." You may think I have put an overly positive spin on the facts. Nevertheless, the evidence based argument unequivocally backs up the fact that a high performance culture is a real possibility, and that real profit performance is linked to the culture of the business.

CHAPTER 13

Asda shopfloor colleagues have the 'final say'

"It's not what you get for work, it's what you become by doing it"

John Ruskin

"With a full century of contrary proof in our possession, and despite our demonstrated capacity for co-operative teamwork, some among us seem to accept the shibboleth of an unbridgeable gap between those who hire and those who are employed. We miserably fail to challenge the lie that what is good for the management is necessarily bad for labour; that for one side to profit, the other must be depressed."

Dwight D. Eisenhower

"Aim at perfection in everything, though in most things it is unattainable. However, they who aim at it, and persevere, will come much nearer to it than those whose laziness and despondency make them give it up as unattainable"

Lord Chesterfield

I wanted to finish this book by giving voice to the Asda colleagues I have met over the years. Every week of my executive life in the Asda business always included a 'listening group' of Asda colleagues, somewhere on my travels. They said some amazing things to me. I think their words bring to life, and give voice to, the concept of 'Asda magic'.

You may have read this book thinking it to be a total 'hegemony', which puts a positive spin on everything. Well, let's hear a sample of what the Asda shop floor colleagues thought of the high performance culture that they worked in. These are their words, not mine:-

Westbrook store of learning
  o "Asda provides stability, it's a friendly team, there is opportunity for development, Asda lives by its values, it provides respect and ethics... there is an upbeat feel about the place... it makes you want to come to work."

Cwmbran store – South Wales
  o "Asda is more open and honest than where I worked before... I started here when I was going through college, and now I'm going on to become a manager."

Cambridge store
  o "I like working for Asda... it's a good company... the managers here do respond, we have tested them."

Clayton Green store – Lancashire
  o "It's a privilege to come to work, I just love it here... we enjoy good rapport with the customers. I left the Asda business for 18 months, but missed

it so much, I just had to come back. This is the best retail company I've ever worked for. It is people friendly."

Eastlands store - Manchester

o "I've been in the business for 22 years, and originally never intended to stay. Asda is the kind of place that develops you through. Retail is very hard work, but it's fun. There is a buzz to it. Asda has created something you want to be part of. If that wasn't the case, I wouldn't have stayed for 22 years."

Sittingbourne store – Kent

o "It's excellent here. We have the best managers. It's friendly, like a family. We have a joke and make it fun."

o "Everyone is treated the same. We're on the same level; people who come here comment about it."

o The work environment is lively, and you want to come to your work."

o "The managers are interested in your life, and you can go and discuss your problems."

Old Kent Road store – London

o "I really appreciate what Asda has done for me. ... picked me off the dole and given me skills... Asda changed my shift to allow me to pick my kids up from school...I can't praise Asda too much."

o "Asda is the best place to work in the UK, and much better than Sainsbury's. Asda are good listeners, and appreciate what you do. I feel like Asda is my own. Sainsbury's don't appreciate you at all."

o "If you are willing to learn, Asda will train you."
o "We tell the store what is really going on, especially if we see people stealing."

Bideford store – Devon

o "I've been in retail for over 30 years, but I love it here. The management team are great here, they listen and respond. Asda is an honourable company, and a great place to work."
o "This store has a real buzz to it, a great atmosphere and is pushing to perform."
o "There is a real team here, we all work together."
o "We are a real family here."
o "This is the only company I've been a part of, where I've enjoyed coming to work."
o "The Asda magic / best welcome really works, because it brings together like-minded people."
o "Work is fun, we enjoy it, and it makes you want to work harder and work together. People want to stay in the tough times, because they want to stick together as a team."
o "You can feel the buzz of the business, it's exciting."
o "One of the big things for me, compared to working at Midland bank, is that communication is done really well. The visuals on the corridor walls and the huddles are very good. I love the huddles because they keep you in the loop as to what's going on, and what you need to know. In the huddles, you are told everything, you are made to feel that you are a part of the business."
o "I'm proud of the company."

Perry Bar store – Birmingham

- "I absolutely love working here. Customers, managers and shopfloor colleagues are my lifelong friends."
- The management team here are very good. You can have a day to day conversation with them,"

Highbridge store – Somerset

- "We have a very friendly company to work for. Managers are very approachable, you get listened to. Things get actioned. I worked for Tesco for 10 years, and Asda is much better to work for. This is a good place to work."
- "Anyone who wants to progress their career can do so."
- "The management team here are great."

Dalgetty Bay store – Scotland

- "The management team here are very supportive, you can approach them easily."
- "This is the best place I've ever worked for praise and appreciation. It makes you feel good when you have worked hard, and it is appreciated."

Newton Abbott store – Devon

- "Customers love this store, they comment on how knowledgeable and friendly the people are. Customers saying we must be paying too much, because we are always smiling."
- "The store feels like a family."
- "I absolutely love it here, after 10 years in Tesco, I already feel more at home after 6 months."

- o "I hated it at Sainsbury's because it felt very 'cliquey', but here colleagues are very friendly and welcoming."
- o "The teams here are very strong. We all help each other when the pressure is on. That's just how it should be."
- o "I've worked for all of them – McDonalds, KFC... none of them have a team spirit like Asda."
- o "We really appreciate what Asda does for us with celebrations."

If you are not moved or impressed by those comments, then there is something wrong with your orientation to people. These are my own undoctored store visit notes taken over a few years of listening. They are not the words of directors talking about the business. These are the words of the people who worked in the stores. Encouragingly, they used words and phrases like 'a great place to work' and 'feels like a family' and 'the buzz', which I would have used. It's great when your words come back to you, from the shopfloor, as observed feelings and behaviours. That's when you know that what you have been trying to achieve through your leaders is having an impact.

In research published by the CIPD, happiness at work was regarded as an important ingredient of the success of a business. Happiness tends to be best in small companies (people feel known / more significant) so Asda certainly 'bucked that trend' as a very large business, which still managed to 'feel' small to its own people. Lack of communication from the top is often cited as a key cause of unhappiness (hence the importance of principle two –

communicate, communicate, communicate). Happiness is also worse, the lower down the organisational hierarchy you are. Yet so many Asda colleagues enjoyed working for Asda (96% in the 2008 engagement survey).

I think the words of the Asda colleagues illustrate the Asda magic that was part of the culture. It is a better illustration of the power of a high performance culture than any words I could use.

CHAPTER 14

Final thoughts

"Treat people as if they were what they ought to be and you help them become what they are capable of becoming."

Johann Wolfgang von Goethe

"In respect to foresight and firmness, the people are more prudent, more stable, and have better judgement than princes."

Niccolo Machiavelli

"Every man's ability may be strengthened or increased by culture"

Sir John Joseph Caldwell Abbott

There are a lot of definitions of culture floating around from the complex:
"The integrated pattern of human behaviour that includes thought, speech, action and artefacts, and depends on the capacity to transmit the knowledge to succeeding generations"

Webster

To the very simple:
"A group's pattern of shared taken-for-granted basic assumptions."

Schein

I really like culture to be described quite simply as 'the way we do things around here'.

Culture is not something for the board only, it is everyone's daily task, it's everyone's job. A business has to talk it, walk it, hire it and live it.

Many businesses resist change to their culture. Some reactions are very overt and noisy, others are covert – where people say, yes but actually mean no. Often people forget to use new ways and processes. The Asda story was given the gift of a 'burning platform'. The business was effectively bankrupt, and everyone at all levels couldn't fail to recognise the need for change. Moreover, all individuals in the top echelons of the company were pretty much changed, to remove any residual hierarchical barriers to change.

Starting from a 'burning platform', with strong leadership to lead change, there was a drive to establish a high performance culture at Asda, over a long and sustained period of time.

Asda also tapped into the spirit of its workforce. Some of the 'Asda magic' emanated from the realisation that individuals have a massive untapped potential. Asda spent a lot of time listening to its people and building their trust. Tapping into people and getting them behind the company mission and purpose, was a major contributor to high performance.

I suppose that the Asda Leadership experience could be described as a pretty good attempt at servant leadership, as described by Robert Greenleaf. Larry Spears, of the Greenleaf Centre, describes ten major attributes of servant leadership. These are:-

o listening
o empathy
o healing
o awareness
o persuasion
o conceptualisation
o foresight
o stewardship
o commitment to the growth of people
o building community

These characteristics are by no means exhaustive, and other gurus have written about vision, integrity, trust and honesty as being important. My point, is that the story of Asda magic encompasses these types of attributes. Asda was a business which walked the talk in the best way it possibly could, with the aim of 'treating people right', with the objective of gaining high performance. It really can be said to have been a 'servant leadership business'.

I hope you have enjoyed the Asda story. It was certainly an exciting 'case study' to live and operate in. I learnt a lot of things about the behaviour of people in organisations along the way. My only hope is that the learning has been expressed in such a way as to benefit others reading this book, in a simple, practical and useable format. Do let me know your impressions via david@davidsmith.uk.com if you would find that helpful.

If you have read this far, well done. So many people are 'textbook collectors'. They seem to buy them as 'shelf trophies', but never really read them. Even less people take any action, as a result of what they read. I'm a pretty avid reader. I know you can subscribe to book summary services, but I tend to write my own book summaries. I find it aids retention of what you are reading.

So now what? Are you going to take any action?

Are you going to change anything in your business which will improve performance?

Who will you enlist as an ally?

If you are the chief executive of your business, how will you share your thoughts with your team?

If you want me to speak to your business board of directors, or to your conference, visit my website at www.davidsmith.uk.com . I would be delighted to tell you more about achieving a high performance culture in your context.

Appendix 1

The origins of Asda in milk / meat / innovation and enterprise

"Success depends in a very large measure upon individual initiative and exertion, and cannot be achieved except by dint of hard work."

Anna Pavlova

"There is no finer investment for any community than putting milk into babies."

Winston Churchill

For those readers who are interested in Asda's history, it would be remiss of me to write about Asda without going back to the very origins of the company. You cannot appreciate a story without putting it into context. When you begin to do the research, there is a fascinating history, some of it full of 'serendipity', but much of it about genuine innovation and certainly a great deal of entrepreneurial flair.

Obviously, I wasn't around in those origins, but my thanks go to Mike Killoran who has been in Asda over 30 years; Gee Singh who came from Mars to Asda and did some meticulous research on the Asda history; and to Tony Campbell who joined Asda in the late 1980s, and was operations and then trading director for many years, for adding a richness to the story I am about to tell.

Asda's origins are in milk production. How can this be, when today you see a huge supermarket business? I suppose the origination point would be the coming of the technology of milk pasteurisation. The technological revolution required an investment in cream separation; milk sterilisation and all the associated equipment. This led to the opening of milk factories in Britain, as farmers began to work together in co-operatives to bring their milk to the market on a large scale.

The movement to factory produced milk started as far back as 1900, but the origins of Asda can be traced to 'Hindell's Dairy Farmers Ltd' in 1920. A group of enterprising dairy farmers from the West Riding of Yorkshire had decided to acquire a wholesale and retail business as an outlet for their milk and related products. The Asda story really begins then, in the 1920s, in the Yorkshire Dales!

At around that time, those farmers set up 'Craven Dairies Ltd', as the first producer of sterilised milk in the Leeds area. One of those farmers was a man called Arthur Stockdale, who operated a milk wholesaling business in the picturesque Yorkshire Dales setting of Grassington. He bought milk from a number of farms in the Yorkshire Dales and then shipped it to the new dairies in Leeds. These were the early days of taking milk to the 'mass market', a thing we take for granted today.

Hindell's Dairy Farmers Ltd went on to buy 'West Riding Milk and Cream Company', along with four shops in Bradford, and Woodlands Dairy. They were also diversifying from the original Leeds dairy into bakery and 16 retail shops in Leeds – 10 of which had cafés attached to them.

There is always a deal of 'serendipity' in business, and Arthur Stockdale, whilst on holiday skiing in Switzerland, happened to meet with a certain Fred Zeigler. Fred Zeigler was a German who lived in the UK, and had built up a number of pork butchers shops. As a result of the holiday relationship, and further meetings, the information gleaned from Fred Zeigler caused Hindell's to further diversify their business into pork. The first pork butchers shop in Leeds in 1928 was a huge success, resulting in a subsidiary company called 'Farm Stores Ltd' being set up in the same year, with Fred Zeigler a significant shareholder. Farm Stores shops made their own sausages; black puddings; boiled hams; roasted pork; cornish pasties; sausage rolls; pork pies and a whole variety of pork based products. With the rapid expansion, these early entrepreneurs decided to move to invest in a meat processing factory. Land was bought at Lofthouse in Yorkshire in 1935 and the factory opened in 1937 to serve the 15 Farm Stores shops. Fred Zeigler was placed in charge of production. By the outbreak of world war two in 1939, there were 17 shops (ten of them bakeries).

Most businesses during the second world war had to learn the rules of regulation by the ministry of food. Britain was at war, and food rationing was the order of the day. The dairies and shops continued to be profitable, but I understand that it was difficult to expand the business at this time, and the decision was taken to invest in land in the early 1940s. This was a method of tax saving at the time, but proved to be a wise long term investment for future expansion capital in later years.

At the end of the second world war, the management felt that the company needed to both modernise and expand. This ambition was beyond the immediate cash flow resources of the business, and capital was raised by offering shares to the general public. This is the first time that the name Associated Dairies appeared. In 1949, the flotation formed a public company called Associated Dairies and Farm Stores Ltd. This new business entity took over Hindell's, and all the dairies and milk companies. Arthur Stockdale was the managing director of the newly formed public company, with holdings of 8 dairies; 2 bakeries; 42 shops; 4 managed farms and 22 rented farms. The geographical trading heartland at that time was Yorkshire, Northumberland and Durham.

The 1950s were the post war years, when Britain was still a pretty austere place. Rationing took some years to unwind, and although the flotation of Associated Dairies had been successful, the ministry of food restrictions continued to make life difficult in the dairy industry. It was not until 1954 that controls on pork were lifted, and Associated Dairies was able to purchase pigs, cattle and sheep to put through the factory in Lofthouse, and also the retail shops.

Milk production continued to be an extremely competitive sector, and the milk marketing board controlled both the production and marketing of all milk after the end of the second world war. The pricing system imposed by the milk marketing board meant that any dairy not producing efficiently would quickly be out of business or taken over by a more efficient producer.

Associated Dairies in the 1950s was working very hard to rationalise and become more efficient than its competitors of the day in the shape of Express Dairies; Northern Dairies and the Leeds Co-operative (who had two thirds of the milk deliveries in the Leeds area). This theme of intense competition and the drive for efficiency became deeply ingrained within the business, and recurs in the future on numerous occasions. Always an environment with thin margins and lots of hard work!

Associated Dairies supplied lots of independent milk rounds in the 1950s, and took a large amount of share from competitor dairies. Associated Dairies also worked hard to rationalise the business on the dairy side, for increased efficiency. At the same time, they expanded the number of pork shops, whilst modernising the cake shops and cafés under the 'Craven Dairies' fascia. By this time, there were 73 pork shops; 29 cake shops / cafés and the rationalised dairy business.

As the reader of this history, you must be thinking that we are almost into the 1960s, and yet this is essentially still milk and meat story, started by Yorkshire Farmers. How on earth did Asda stores arise from this unlikely background?

The answer lies not with Arthur Stockdale, but his son Noel (who was later to become Sir Noel Stockdale). Noel met and struck up an immediate rapport with the

Asquith brothers, and this was another piece of business 'serendipity' similar to Noel's father meeting Fred Zeigler on holiday many years earlier.

Peter Asquith was a butcher by trade, and his brother Fred was a teacher. Peter was typically humourous about their occupations. "In our family the bright ones became teachers, and the rest were butchers". Peter was never arrogant, but he was, above all things, an ideas man and he had a good eye for business success. The Asquith family business was called W.R. Asquith, of Pontefract, and comprised butchers shops and mobile vans delivering meat to households. The Pontefract store struggled badly. Their idea was to create a 'self service' supermarket, where customers would pick goods from the shelves themselves, rather than being served to fill their order. This was 'cutting edge' retail in 1958.

The Asquiths hit on the idea of a means to offer value for money for customers through their buyer Jack Hewitt, who ordered 1000 cans of soup; utilising a voucher scheme being run at the time by Crosse and Blackwell. Crosse and Blackwell were offering a 6 old pence postal order for every soup label sent to their factory. Jack Hewitt and the Asquiths cut the labels off the cans and claimed their £600 from Crosse and Blackwell. They used the cash to offer their customers 6 old pence off, and 'value' was born as a retail 'mechanic'. Peter and Fred sold this successful store to Thrift in 1960 for £50,000 with retail experience under their belt. The Asquiths then started another store in 1963 by converting an old ex-cinema in Castleford, which had been called 'The Queens'. The advantage of this site was that it was adjacent to a large municipal car park. Peter Asquith was aware that car ownership was growing in the early 1960s, and customers would begin to drive to shop and go home with shopping in the car boot, a real potential 'step change' from small basket daily shopping, utilising public transport or simply walking. Peter was a retail visionary, early into self service, and quick to spot the opportunity for retail revolution with the advent of car ownership for the masses. The Queens supermarket opened in May 1963, with self service groceries, and an arcade of shops for fresh food. The format offered 'permanent reductions' as its proposition for customers.

A second store of 5000 square feet was added in 1964 in Edlington. This had been a traditional market, with stalls originally. By 1965 Peter Asquith was building the first new build supermarket, at South Elmsall, near Pontefract, on the site of the old Palace cinema. All these stores were branded 'Queens' after the cinema name from the first store. They also all had large car parks attached to them.

The driving idea behind 'Queens', other than self service, and ample parking, was to give 14% to 17% off normal prices. There were no special offers, but permanent reductions. At this early stage, the Asquiths and Jack Hewitt had hit on the powerful force of value in driving customer loyalty. Jack Hewitt eventually became managing director of Asda, but in the early days he was responsible for the buying and selling; whilst Fred looked after the administration of the business; and Peter Asquith, 'the ideas man', went in search of new stores.

Retail price maintenance was very much in force in the Britain of the early 1960s, and many manufacturers refused to supply the 'Queens' stores for fear of upsetting their high street accounts. Cadburys; Beechams and Polycell all refused to sell to the Asquiths, whilst Carnation Milk; Kelloggs; Typhoo Tea and Campbells Soup would only deliver via wholesale businesses. Despite this, the format was massively successful.

Now the two parts of this retail history converge. The Asquiths were riding the wave of a very successful and innovative retail format. These were larger out of town stores; open until 8.00pm; self service; with adjacent car parking facilities and driven by value – permanently low prices which were substantially lower than the prevailing market. However, despite the strong cash flow and huge success, the Asquiths were stretched financially and administratively in expanding to acquire new sites.

At the same time, we return to the story of Associated Dairies. By 1965, they were very keen to diversify the portfolio from the restrictions in the milk market. Peter Asquith was looking for a company to take over his in store butchers operation at Queens, and it made sense to contact Associated Dairies.

The meeting between Peter Asquith and Noel Stockdale is the stuff of legend. This was the birth of the Asda business in 1965. Controversy remains over whether the Asda name is short for Associated Dairies, or an abbreviation of Asquith and Dairies. Either way, the name Asda came to the market, and Associated Dairies had the cash flow from its milk and meat businesses, and the capital from the land investments made in the war years, to enable the much required retail expansion of the combined business.

This was milk and meat, meeting innovation in retail. Both companies had a philosophy of hard work and enterprise. As Peter Asquith said "none of this would have happened if it hadn't been for Noel." Noel was not only impressed with Peter Asquith's supermarkets, he also had the vision to see Associated Dairies expansion into supermarkets.

The real foundations of the Asda philosophy were laid in 1965. The South Elmsall store opened in September of that year with Peter Asquith pronouncing "how often do you find a car park on your doorstep? People with cars will be able to drive to the park, walk through the store, and pack their cars with groceries, instead of having to carry them any distance". This will certainly seem second nature to readers now, but in 1965, everything was fragmented around the high street in every town and city in Britain. This was innovation in retailing.

The trading philosophy was also set in 1965. Peter Asquith declared that "nothing we sell will be at full, normally expected prices. Our aim is to sell as much as possible at a smaller margin, rather than less at a larger profit. That is to the mutual benefit of the housewife and ourselves".

The next piece of retail innovation came via a phenomenon called the 'GEM' stores. A major US retailer, Government Exchange Mart (GEM) had expanded internationally, and bought two very large stores in the UK. GEM's first site was an 80,000 square foot store in West Bridgeford, Nottingham. They then acquired a second site in Crossgates, Leeds. Both Sainsbury (then the number one grocery retailer in the UK) and Tesco had turned down these sites. Both stores were losing money, but Peter Asquith was convinced he could make them pay. The Asda team visited GEM's head office in St. Louis in the USA, and negotiated a deal to buy the stores for 20% of whatever Asda could recoup from the inland revenue as tax losses. Asda negotiated with the revenue to recoup the £320,000 losses, and so acquired the stores without any cash layout! This was one spectacular deal, and the Nottingham store opened with Asda's retailing skills, taking £30,000 per week, when it had only been taking barely £6,000 per week as a GEM store.

Tony Campbell, (Asda's operations director, then trading director for many years), who was working for Fine Fare at the time, remembers shopping in the West Bridgeford store back in its early days. "It was revolutionary. Everything was discounted. There was one long row of checkouts, the fresh food was concessioned out, and Asda operated the core grocery & non food. There was nothing like it at the time. Everything else was on a smaller scale and high street based"

The acquisition of the GEM stores by Asda in those early days was retail revolution. It led to a complete reappraisal of what a big a supermarket could be. Traditional wisdom had said 5,000 – 20,000 square feet, whereas the Asda vision moved that to 40- 60,000 square feet. This radical insight gave Asda a massive lead over its major rivals, who were locked into smaller high street sites. Out of town retailing had begun in Britain in earnest.

You could say with certainty that Asda was the innovator around the concept of 'one stop shopping.' At this time, petrol filling stations were added as part of the one stop shop. This was a follow up to one of Peter Asquith's earlier ideas. In 1959 in his first supermarket in Pontefract, he had turned an old malt kiln site into a petrol filling station. Peter wanted to discount petrol, but none of the oil companies would supply him. In the end, Peter did a deal with the Russian oil company, Nafta, for discounted fuel.

By 1969 Asda had opened its 24th store in Pudsey, Leeds, with 52,000 square feet of selling space, and parking for over 1,000 cars. The foundation of the Asda formula was set. Asda was about one stop shopping in larger stores than its competitors, there was parking and petrol on site, goods were discounted to give great value to customers. The non food departments were developed over a period of time, and had very shaky beginnings. There was no one in the organisation who had any non food experience, but food was doing sufficiently well at the time, it gave the business the time and space to learn the hard way.

In 1970, Asda had over 30 stores, and the group had managed a successful transition from a dairy company with some retail interests, into a discount supermarket group with dairy interests. The serendipity which produced this was the entrepreneurial spirit of the Asquith brothers, and in particular Peter as the ideas man, together with the solid financials of the established dairy group, Associated Dairies under Noel Stockdale.

However, by the early 1970s, the Asquith Brothers had sold their interest in Asda Stores Ltd, as it became a wholly owned subsidiary of associated dairies. The group appointed Peter Firmston – Wlliams as managing director of Asda Stores Ltd, an experienced professional retailer. He presided over the growth of the Asda business for 10 years until 1981, as Asda moved both north to Scotland, but also south to Birmingham, London and the West Country.

Asda rode the wave of out of town shopping expansion by car borne people, and by 1981 when Peter Firmston-Williams left the Group, there were 80 stores and 3 million square feet of selling space, with the majority trading six days a week. The only downbeat note at this time, was that Peter Asquith also decided to leave his position as a director of Associated Dairies, and set up his own property company, and have a go at DIY retailing. Peter did not have the same success in DIY as he had in food and general merchandise, but by 1980 the scale of the Asda retailing miracle was widely acknowledged in business circles. A management horizon report in 1980 assessed Asda as "the most profitable retailing group in the country, with the second highest stock turn, and sales per square foot."

At this point, the story of Asda turns from amazing success, innovation and the time of the entrepreneurs, to the turbulent years of the 1980's. This is an altogether different period in the history of Asda.

Appendix 2

The turbulent times for Asda in the 1980's

> "If you can keep your head, when all about you are losing theirs and blaming it on you. If you can trust yourself when all men doubt you, but make allowance for their doubting too; if you can meet with triumph and disaster and treat those two imposters the same"
>
> Rudyard Kipling
>
> "He that will not apply new remedies must expect new evils; for time is the greatest innovator"
>
> Francis Bacon

Looking back, Asda had been heading for trouble for a while. The expansion southwards, and the acquisition of Allied retailers in 1978 had both been profit dilutive, and there had been a sharp drop in both sales growth and net margins. In the 1981 annual report, Sir Noel Stockdale pointed out "it is evident from the published figures that the steepest downturn in profits occurred in Allied retailers, caused by the integration of Williams furniture with Wades, coupled with the enormous pre-opening expenses incurred in the development of the Bowland Olympia store." Turnover was experiencing a slowdown in 1981, in contrast to growth of between 30% and 50% per year throughout the 1970's. The 1981 increase of

19% in turnover was only 5% above inflation, and the 3% increase in profits were the lowest ever in the history of Asda.

Some of this was a legacy of experimentation throughout the dynamic growth of the 1970's. Asda formed a travel company (Asda travel); Sandmartin was commenced: an idea to acquire smaller fresh food stores in smaller towns and was abandoned because it did not work; an electrical goods wholesale business then ran into difficulty on the change from purchase tax to VAT and was disposed of by a management buy out; Wades – an upmarket furniture and carpet retailer was acquired in 1977; Allied retailers – a carpet and furniture group was acquired in 1978. The Asda business struggled with these acquisitions. Some were disposed of in the 1970's, but the furniture and carpet businesses were a 'millstone' around the neck of the company during the 1980's, as the economy took a turn for the worse.

This diversification strategy for Asda, constantly searching for new growth vehicles to replicate the success in innovation of the early days, proved largely unviable.

John Fletcher was appointed chief executive in 1981, and faced an altogether tougher situation. The economy was slowing down, and unemployment was rising. Customers were spending less. John Fletcher decided to increase margins on branded foods to improve profitability. His view was that Asda had chased sales at the expense of profitability. He could have developed an 'own label' product line to improve profitability, but he felt such a move would be too late compared to the advantage of Sainsbury and Tesco in this area, and that Asda would suffer huge losses if it took time to develop own label products.

During John Fletcher's 3 years as chief executive, he did significantly improve short term profitability, but some of that profit came from increased prices, and it began to disenfranchise customers. Those customers had trusted Asda to be the best value store in their area over a whole range of goods. The disputes at board level over the consequences of this change of strategy meant that he left Asda in 1984.

At this time, Asda had multiple difficulties:- the problems in the furniture and carpet businesses; the difficult economic climate; and the loss of the discount price position – but there was another threat on Asda's horizon. This was the period when Tesco and Sainsbury both realised that the out of town superstore formula was correct; and they began to aggressively compete for every potential site that became available.

This was the making of a 'perfect storm' for Asda. Growth was slowing; the economy was tough; the business had diversified into unprofitable furniture and carpet businesses; the price advantage had been lost, and competitors were on the march to copy Asda's strategy.

John Hardman, who had been John Fletcher's finance director, succeeded him as chief executive in 1984. The market research which greeted John Hardman on his appointment did not make 'pretty' reading. The customers said that Asda's stores were 'dull and tired' when compared with Tesco and Sainsbury, and this view was more firmly held in the south. The expansion southward had proven extremely expensive for Asda, was not yielding the required level of return on the investment, and customers in the south in particular were very loyal to own label brands in Waitrose, Sainsbury, Tesco and Marks & Spencer. There were other factors coming out of the research, in that customers were saying that service; cleanliness; the wider product range, and ease of shop were very important to them in deciding where to shop. These were all issues for Asda at the time.

John Hardman and the board of Asda adopted a three pronged approach based upon the research. Firstly, they commissioned a design company (Fitch & Co) to invent a customer focused design solution to improve the 'feel' of the Asda stores. This was aimed to improve: layout; lighting; decoration; uniforms and external signage. The concept they came up with was piloted in a new store in Leamington Spa in 1985. The concept had a non food browsing area; dramatic displays of fresh food and an 'easy to shop' packaged grocery area. The look was colour coded with pastel shades.

Secondly, the Asda board announced an ambitious move into developing 1,000 own label products, in an attempt to offer better value to customers, and match the march stolen by Tesco and Sainsbury. By the end of 1987, they had over 3,000 lines launched, which was a substantial step change, from a standing start.

Thirdly, John Hardman instituted a major customer initiative. He ordered that every customer complaint should go direct to him, and that there should be a customer service programme for every operator facing the customer. He also improved facilities for employees at the back of house, and began issuing monthly prizes for service performance.

At the same time as these 3 major strategies, John Hardman began a process of modernising and centralising distribution. Up until this point, all deliveries to stores had been direct to the back door of every store, by every individual supplier. Many retailers were moving to centralised distribution operations, to gain logistics efficiency through 'cross docking' and sending one mixed load to the store, rather than multiple single stream deliveries. This was the right strategy, but implemented at probably the worst time. Asda was facing the 'perfect storm' of economic downturn; increasing competition and a store format that needed updating. Changing to centralise distribution at that time was a major piece of disruption and change, which would have been better suited to a thriving rather than a struggling business.

Tony Campbell remembers the time very well because he joined Asda as operations director to implement the store renewal programme. He comments "the plan to turn the business around was not all wrong, but it was certainly beyond the capability of the team of the day to implement it. Some of the elements were wrong. The new store format had upmarket fixtures and marble counters, whilst not much had been done about produce and meat quality. The shops looked more expensive, and were more expensive, because prices were drifting upwards. Prices were probably at parity with Tesco at best."

Tony's view was very clear "not all the things being done went badly. The own label strategy worked brilliantly well, and that business began to fly. There were just not enough good things happening." At that time, not only was competition intensifying from Tesco and Sainsbury, but Morrison's and Kwik Save were also doing well. All this was attacking Asda's sales growth potential, in its heartland in the north, at that time.

These trading difficulties coincided with one further piece of diversification which was to prove unsuccessful. The Asda board decided to merge with MFI (Mullard Furniture Industries) in 1985, and this was heralded as a £2 billion 'marriage' which was a launch pad for major expansion. The Financial Times commented that "such is the scale of retailing now, that the way ahead for both appears to be a marriage of convenience to bring together their huge resources needed to compete in the 1990's."

Work commenced in 1987 to build seven new distribution centres, and they became operational in 1989. Although this was the right thing to do for the long term, this was a huge and disruptive undertaking for any business, and certainly for an Asda which was not in great shape at the time.

As if all this was not enough, at the same time, Asda moved its head office from an old converted mill in Morley near Leeds, to a new build state of the art complex in the centre of Leeds. Asda house was opened by Margaret Thatcher in 1987, at a cost of £15 million. At any other time, this would have been a prestigious project, but moving head office at a time when Asda was heading for its darkest hour, was another piece of unnecessary distraction.

Having successfully sold MFI in 1987, David Donne relinquished his short term chairmanship, and John Hardman became both chairman and chief executive. The managing director's post was split jointly between Tony Campbell, who had joined as operations director in 1985, and Graham Stow who joined as personnel director in 1984. The Asda board, at this time, decided to focus purely on the core retailing business, and dispose of interests in the carpet and furniture division (Allied) and its fresh food division (Associated Fresh Foods). But, before any of these decisions could be enacted, another element added to the 'perfect storm' for Asda.

A financial 'hurricane' swept through the world's money markets – 'Black Monday' occurred on 19th October 1988. This had the effect of sabotaging any potential deal to dispose of Allied, and Asda had to continue to manage these businesses, although they were an increasing drain on the core, both financially, and in diverting both management time and focus.

If all this was not enough, what else could the reader think of to add to this potentially lethal cocktail? So far we have listed a demand downturn; intensifying competition; loss of focus on the price gap which was so dangerous for a discount retailer; struggling investments in the south of the UK; a store format that wasn't quite right; major disruptive change to centralise distribution and a financial crisis in markets scuppering the opportunity to remove financially underperforming parts of the group.

The last thing Asda needed in 1989 was a major systems change. Big systems programmes are famous for causing large businesses to go 'off the rails' in their own right, let alone when a 'perfect storm' is taking place. Yet in the 1980's Asda implemented electronic point of sale (EPOS) in all the stores, opening a dedicated purpose built computer processing centre (at Westbank) in Leeds in 1989, adjacent to the newly built Asda house headquarters.

By 1989, the 'perfect storm' had built to a crescendo. The capital investment for the push to build new stores in the south; together with aggressive 'catch up' expansion of own label products; the cost of renewal of stores to the new 'Fitch' design concept, all served to push up Asda's costs. This pressure also pushed up Asda's gross margin, making the discount price position versus competitors much less marked.

It seems there was little (other than the origin of the Asda own label brand) to see as a positive, in the Asda of the 1980's. However, there was one jewel in the rather tarnished crown. That was the launch of a new range of fashion clothing, designed for all the family, into 65 stores during 1989. Asda took a 20% interest in the George Davies partnership. George Davies had ended his relationship with the Next retail business, and was looking for a new partner. The George clothing brand at Asda was an almost overnight success, and strong growth took place almost from the inception, reinforcing the concept of 'one stop shopping'. This was one area which would later contribute in a major way to Asda's resurgence, but more of that later.

The final 'nail in the coffin' during Asda's 'perfect storm' was the bid for 61 Gateway stores in 1989. Asda had been slowly discarding the brand values of the business, embodied in its original 'value for money' proposition, and getting into a 'doom loop' of rising costs and having to raise margins and prices to balance the books. John Hardman did the Gateway acquisition deal for £705 million, and the city view was that Asda had paid too much for the stores. However, the internal view was that the average purchase price of £11.6 million per store was considerably lower than the average £16.3 million it had cost Asda to buy land, and build the 13 stores Asda had opened in 1988. The internal company view was that the Isocoles/ Gateway deal would strengthen Asda's national store position, at a significantly lower cost, and in a much shorter time scale than it would have taken to grow organically. The deal took Asda's retail total selling space from 5.1 million to 7.6 million square feet, and increased the number of stores by 30% from 131 to 192.

Tony Campbell remembers that time very clearly. "It all seemed very unlikely that the Gateway deal would happen. The detail had not been worked out, such as the requirement for expanded distribution capacity. Distribution had just taken on the 'herculean' task of centralisation, and here was a proposal to plug in 30% more volume, with no additional warehouse capacity" Tony was dispatched, along with John Miller, to negotiate the management agreement as to what would happen to the Gateway stock on the store shelves, and how the shops would be converted. Tony reflects "in the end, we produced a plan and got on with it. The Gateway stock on the shelves was taken away; Asda refurbished the stores; and they progressively reopened, with Asda stock on the shelf, on conversion day"

But, despite taking on this massive acquisition project, it was a dark time for Asda. John Hardman commented in the 1990 annual report "the group has produced disappointing results.....profit in the year to April 1990 fell to £180.3 million"

This was in stark contrast to the previous year, where profits had been £246.6 million. The increased borrowings to finance the Gateway acquisition coincided with dramatically higher interest rates in the economy. This resulted in a dramatic fall in interest earnings of £34.5 million in 1989, to a net interest payment of £29.9 million in 1990. The high interest rates (14%) were not only hurting Asda. The UK housing market collapsed at the same time, and hurt the non food side of the Asda business, together with a dramatic fall in the contribution of Allied Maples from £30.2 million in 1989, to only £5.2 million in 1990. Meanwhile, Tony Campbell's foreboding about how well the newly centralised distribution would cope with 30% more volume without additional capacity, resulted in a £16 million cost to the profit & loss account.

The recession in the economy and the poorly timed acquisition had turned the £1 billion cash surplus of 1987, into £1 billion of debt by 1990. Asda was heading quickly for potentially breaching its bank covenants. Tony Campbell remembers it as a time of paralysis. "Everyone was seized with inaction at the centre. The conversion of the Gateway stores was going well, but the mounting debt issue was the problem. At this time, there was a move against the board by the shareholders. Scottish Widows were a major shareholder, who made a statement that they did not trust the current leadership of Asda. The non executive directors instituted a major review of the board, via Whitehead Mann. Sir Godfrey Messervy and Kenneth Morton were the non executive directors who led that review."

At the same time, Asda reported "the effect of high interest rates has significant implications for the group.... reflecting the full year effect of borrowings incurred to fund the Gateway store purchase." The Asda group profit fell again to £172.8 million, whilst the net interest payments now stood at £85.5 million. The contribution from Allied Marples fell even further to £1.6 million.

The company share price at that time was floundering, and both John Hardman and Graham Stowe resigned in June 1991. Sir Godfrey Messervey, chairman of Costain group, who had been a non executive director of Asda since 1986, became caretaker chairman of Asda. Richard Harker, the managing director of Allied Maples and Tony Campbell became joint managing directors. At this very dark hour in Asda's history, there was one final tragedy to unfold. Sir Godfrey Messervy suffered a heart attack and had to step down as caretaker chairman. Frank Knight, who had been at United Biscuits, was appointed as deputy chairman, and set about the task of finding a new chairman.

Patrick Gillam, who had retired as number two at BP, was appointed in September 1991. Patrick was also deputy chairman at Standard Chartered bank. Tony Campbell remembers Patrick arriving. He and Patrick went around the shareholders together. Shareholders were very angry. Tony recalls that their general message was very clear "you need to appoint a new chief executive, and it won't be from the current team." The shareholders had lost a fortune, and concern was running high.

So ended the turbulent years of Asda in the 1980s. The retail innovator, the champion of value and discounting had been brought to its knees. Asda was in need of a major turnaround, and there was a very real risk that it would cease to exist as an entity. Bankruptcy was 'knocking at the door'.

APPENDIX 3

The Asda turnaround/ renewal & breakout: the 1990's

> "Believe each day that has dawned is your last. Some hour to which you have not been looking forward will prove lovely"
>
> Horace

> "If you can talk with crowds and keep your virtue,
> or walk with kings - nor lose the common touch,
> If neither foes nor loving friends can hurt you,
> If all men count with you but not too much;
> If you can fill the unforgiving minute with sixty seconds worth of distance run,
> Yours is the earth and everything in it,
> and – which is more – you'll be a man my son!"
>
> Rudyard Kipling

> "The universe is transformation; our life is what our thoughts make it"
>
> Marcus Aurelius

The story of Asda's turnaround commenced with the announcement at the end of 1991 that Archie Norman, the then finance director at Kingfisher, would be appointed as chief executive. Archie was a Harvard MBA who had become the youngest partner at

McKinsey consulting, and then became group finance director at Kingfisher, which made him the youngest director of a FTSE100 company, at 32 years of age.

When Archie arrived in Leeds as the newly appointed chief executive of Asda, on a dark day just after Christmas, he was facing a herculean task. The company had lost all direction and momentum; the share price had fallen to a paltry 27p per share; there was a debt mountain of £1billion; and the business was experiencing the real risk of breaching its bank covenants. Meltdown was a distinct possibility, if the crisis was not quickly averted.

Archie's first action was to pull together his top team. Allan Leighton had agreed to join Asda as marketing director. Allan was 39 years old at the time, and was a Mars 'veteran'. His role before joining Asda was as sales director of Pedigree pet foods. The combination of Archie's strategic skills and Allan's dynamism and communication abilities, were to prove immensely powerful in the turnaround of Asda. Archie also hired Phil Cox as his finance director, and made Tony Campbell, (the only survivor of John Hardman's board), his trading director. The business ran with these four key players, but it was a very 'dangerous' time in those early days. The business future of Asda was far from secure.

Allan recalls one of his first meetings, where the gathered consultants were recommending that the only logical way forward was to break up and sell off the business, to other players in the market. "My reaction was that I had come to turn around the business, not to give in and sell it off." As we now know, that is what happened, but the demise of Asda was viewed as a very real possibility by analysts at the time. Tony Campbell remembers that dark time very clearly. "The business was in limbo for what seemed like ages. But when Archie came, he had something about him. He gave direction, and had determination. The business ran with four players at the top and it was very much 'forged in the fire'. A lot of action was generated, to get momentum, and break out of the inertia which had gripped the business. The view was that if enough momentum was created, some things would begin to work".

Archie forged a clear vision from his 'day zero'. He had inherited a bankrupt business; with poor systems; a hierarchical organisation with a head office which was 'silo' driven, and disconnected from the stores.

Archie believed that Asda needed to get back to its original purpose – its core values – the price advantage had to be regained, customers had to be served with real personality, and the business had to be renewed in every area – stores, management and culture.

However, the first major actions had to halt the financial crisis, and a shareholder emergency rights issue of £350 million took place, in conjunction with an immediate company wide pay freeze. Everything that could be done to avert bankruptcy was being done. The national union officials were supportive of the pay freeze, but the local regional officials disobeyed this view and called for a strike to protest at the pay freeze, causing the Asda board directors to make a visit to every single store, in order to explain 'first hand' to people on the shop floor just how

desperate things were. Asda employees were told of the
need for everyone to 'cut their cloth' for the survival of
the Asda business. The ultimate vote by Asda workers
was not to take any strike action, and this was a
powerful step in Asda beginning to talk directly with its
workforce, about all challenges facing the business,
rather than through a third party in the shape of the
trade union.

Having averted the 'doom loop' of the financial crisis, at
least for a time, the new team began to formulate the
strategy of the 'virtuous circle', based upon Archie
Norman's vision for the Asda business. The 'virtuous
circle' entailed: getting back to price competitiveness;
which was paramount in restoring customer flow into
the stores; which would in turn reduce the fixed cost
percent to sales; higher volumes would give better
trading terms; which would in turn give scope to lead
a breakthrough in store productivity and range
redirection.

Archie communicated a clear statement of his vision for
the business to get back into growth, via a three year
'recovery plan'. 'Recovery' encapsulated a plan to shed
the elements of the business acquired in the 1980's,
which were not part of the core business, and therefore
assist Asda in 'pulling back' from the financial precipice.
'Recovery' also involved the direct communication to
everyone in the business a new purpose 'to satisfy the
weekly shopping needs of ordinary working people and
their families who demand value'. Asda was back to
chasing its original mission; of being 'Britain's best value
food & clothing superstore'. The 'recovery plan'

encapsulated the desire to create a new business culture, enabling people in the organisation to deliver the strategy. This sounds somewhat prosaic, but it was vital that people in the business were mobilised to deliver. Asda, like many other retailers, had developed a military management style which was very much 'command and control'. Retail as a sector was very hierarchical in the 1990s, and very much directed by a 'tell & do' style. Asda was very much a 'status driven' management. The head office at Asda house had become 'silo' driven within functions, and did not exist to serve the stores. Indeed, it had become mired in the type of bureaucracy which so often grips large organisations. The desire to change this became known as establishing a new 'Asda way of working' (AWW).

The 'Asda way of working' was the nomenclature for a new direction for business leadership. The Asda business needed to become more stores centric. The stores needed to become the 'heroes', having more 'say' in product mix and space allocation for customers. Asda house, in Leeds, was charged with becoming more responsive to the needs of the stores, and satisfying the needs of customers.

The galvanising force within the 'Asda way of working' was the shared direction of six values, which were to be the 'backdrop' of everything done by the people in the business. These six values were:-

- o "We are all colleagues – one team"
  (this was emphasising removal of hierarchy and status in the business...the feeling that everyone in

the boat should have an oar and be rowing the boat)

o "Selling is our universal responsibility"
(this was about getting sales growth going again...the lifeblood of any retail business...shared by all, not just the stores themselves)

o "What we sell is better value"
(This was going back to Asda's core 'raison d'etre', being better value than everyone else... the way Peter Asquith and Noel Stockdale had originally positioned Asda Stores Ltd . The business had to get back to offering customers a substantial discount over rivals for the same quality)

o "Through selling we make our service legendary"
(This was the 'personality' of the business, being allowed to shine through to the customers. The aim was for Asda colleagues to be famous for 'warmth', friendliness and product knowledge)

o "We hate waste of any kind"
(This was to emphasise that to be an every day low price retailer, Asda had to be the lowest cost retailer, in order to be able to fund the investment)

o "We all need to improve the business every day in every way"
(Continuous improvement was a watchword from Japanese companies, and Asda wanted to gain momentum by taking everyone's ideas for improving business performance from the shop floor upwards).

This was the cultural re-birth of Asda. The business determined to get rid of the barriers between management and 'staff', with everyone wearing a badge with their first name, and everyone was to call everyone else a 'colleague'. The new values were to literally be a new 'way of working', not just words on a notice on the wall.

The poignancy of all this was that the business was on its knees, literally at the financial 'cliff edge' and about to fall. The proposed new way forward... a chance for survival......... consequently had some early adopters, though this was not universally the case. Tony Campbell recalls "there was something about that early time which made the business 'hearing' so acute, and something about the pressure to survive was so intense, that it was possible to create something new".

Archie Norman remembers the turnaround at Asda as an event which fitted its time. "People were looking for a workplace community. Will my boss treat me with respect? If people don't want to do things they won't. People tend to ask the question... is this a worthwhile thing to do? Affiliation matters to people. They want to belong... whether that means family; football club or the Asda business. People also want to think of themselves as doing something worthwhile. The ethics of business matter more and more. Growing earnings per share and financial performance are inputs, not outputs. Meeting the needs of customers is the real thing, and profits will flow. You have to develop affiliation and a cause. People will work hard in that context."

Asda in the early 1990's worked hard to create a very different environment from 'just do as you're told' traditional retail. It was very much about creating a cause – providing the best value in the market place for customers – and a framework in which people could perform. Reserved parking spaces for management were removed from all Asda sites and cars were parked not by status, but on a first come first served basis. The internal office walls came down in Asda house, with everyone sitting in open plan. Asda began to have a very different 'feel' to it. This is much more common in businesses today, but in the early 1990s it was a 'revolution'. Archie Norman's view of the business in those early days was that "Asda was a broken business and turnaround began as a 'burning platform'. These conditions are harder to replicate elsewhere."

There was a real need to harness that 'burning platform' as the atmosphere and springboard for change. 'Corporate renewal' became the delivery vehicle for moving the business forward. A 'renewal team' was formed with cross functional representation from all areas of the business. The deliberate intent was to break traditional functional boundaries, creating freedom to take risks and innovate. It was a deliberate attack on functional 'silos'.

'Store renewal' was a desperate need in Asda stores at that time, since the store real estate had become 'tired'. But there was very little capital expenditure available, because of the financially precarious state of the business. The cash limit for physical renewal of the store fabric was £2 million per store (compared with an industry average of £5-10 million at the time), and the need was to radically change the space given to departments in store. The aim was to give more emphasis to fresh food (produce/bakery/meat). Because of the financial constraints on renewal, a strategy was developed to transform the management style in stores, to conform to the six new values and the 'Asda way of working'. By developing a more involving and participative style of management with colleagues in stores, the main idea was that the business would aim for a sales uplift arising from better customer service.

The very first renewal store was Wolstanton in the west midlands. The store had minimal capital expenditure, with some changes to layout emphasising fresh foods. The major difference came through the people and the culture of the store, rather than the cost of physical change. This was an ordinary store, with a typical management team and a typical store manager. Colleagues at the store were listened to, and involved in the whole renewal project for their store. Regular daily communication began, giving them information about how the renewal was performing. They were also briefed about the importance of great customer service, through selling with personality. They felt 'in the loop' on the whole project. The whole process also involved listening to customers as well as listening to colleagues. Customers were given the final say in any matters of layout, where there was conflict between the renewal team and the local store.

At the same time, the renewal team went to different retailers around the world, searching for new ideas to create excitement in the store. That tour was where the idea of an 'egg shack' with a thatched roof came from, with a button for the children to create the sound of a cockerel crowing.

The security gates were taken out of the foyer at Wolstanton, giving customers open access to the shop floor. Fixture height was lowered to give better 'line of sight' into the store, and customers were met with fresh fruit and vegetables in abundance 'first in flow', to tempt them to start their shopping experience. There was more emphasis on fresh food around the store, with hand carved hams on the deli counter, and freshly baked bread throughout the day. Walls were knocked down along the store 'back wall' so that customers could see colleagues preparing fresh food, whereas preparation was previously done behind closed doors.

The effect of 'theatre' and the 'feel' was created by the Asda colleagues' selling activity, creating a 'whirlwind' success in Wolstanton . The store achieved a substantial 60% increase in sales, and resulted in Archie Norman's board committing to roll out the low cost programme for renewal to 40 stores across the UK. The model was to be low capital, but high emphasis on changing the culture in those stores.

The capital expenditure commitment was £80 million, but the desire to roll out the 'Asda way of working' was in many senses a much bigger change. This was a much needed physical store renewal programme, but the 'cultural renewal' was more significant. Asda was in effect getting closer to its customers. The combination was dynamite, and as a consequence, all 40 store renewals achieved similar uplifts to those seen in Wolstanton. The programme was renewing the retail culture, whilst also physically moving the Asda stores forward as far as capital constraints allowed.

Asda committed to the 'renewal' of the whole chain as the 1990's unfolded, and it became clear that Asda was going back to its core mission of providing great value to customers, whilst giving an exciting 'selling and service' experience at the same time. Bringing the 'Asda way of working' to life provided fabulous trading results, and showed the energy that could be released by getting colleagues involved in their business. It was employee engagement in action.

> Archie Norman: "at times, you have to do things which seem counter cultural. You have to get the required efficiency and energy, and do it without making people feel bad. People outside Asda didn't understand what we were trying to do. It was not about a load of 'initiatives'. You have to really 'get it' and embrace it, or it won't fly. Nothing succeeds on one idea."

By the end of Archie's first year as CEO, the £1 billion debt had reduced to £76 million and sales volumes were up by 27%. The turnaround of the Asda business had begun in earnest. Asda had rediscovered its core values, and customers returning to Asda stores were finding a revitalised business. They were seeing the 'Asda price' differential again, and they were 'pocketing the difference'. Allan Leighton was leading the renewal team, and that dynamism and clear communication flair, for which Allan is famous, was making a real difference to the commercial results of the business.

There was a variety of experimentation under way in Asda alongside the rollout of the 'renewal 'programme. One of the features of food retailing in the early 1990's, was the emergence of the foreign owned hard discount chains destined to 'nibble away' at the 'soft underbelly' of grocery retailing in the UK. Asda launched two new formats at this time, in the shape of Asda Dales and the value stores. Both were designed to produce even keener value to customers through lower costs. Asda Dales was positioned as the best discount operation in the country. The stores had limited range of 7,000 products versus a standard Asda of 22,000 product lines, and a much smaller management team, whilst offering a wide range of fresh foods. In those early days of the 1990's, those stores recorded 60% uplift, and more than successfully competed with the likes of Aldi and Netto.

Not only was Asda experimenting with formats in the early 1990's but there was innovation in the ways of working all around the business. This amounted to doing different things in the Leeds head office – Asda house. Ten positive action groups (PAG's) were set up by the board, with the same technique as setting up the 'renewal team'. Individuals were selected from across functional boundaries, to work on major challenges for the Asda business, with the objective of making changes which would impact total chain performance. The subjects of those positive action groups tended to be a revitalisation of a particular product category (produce/ frozen foods). They examined Asda's market share; performance compared to competitors; how customers shopped the category and examined customer perception of the Asda offer in that category.

These cross functional work groups were part of the 'renewal' for Asda house culture, and they became such 'hot houses' of radical review and new ideas, that they eventually became known as 'saunas'. There was some 'heat' applied to the problems of moving the business forward. There was a resulting improvement in category sales performance, as each group reached a conclusion, and also the silo boundaries of Asda house were broken down. The whole business began to pull together to raise performance. Everyone in the business; whether in store renewals; the value and Asda Dales discount stores; or in Asda house 'saunas', began to realise the potential which could be achieved by everyone doing their 'bit' to turn around the company performance.

This was a real sense of a pioneering spirit to save the company. As Archie remarks "don't see this as a 'menu' of tactics, but as a composite whole." The composite momentum in store sales, and the transformation at the centre, meant that by 1993 the debt 'mountain' had gone, and the Asda group was £4.2 million cash positive. This turnaround was a huge tribute to the original team Archie pulled together, and the determination to renew the Asda business through the 3 year recovery plan.

I joined the business in March 1994, at just that moment when Asda was beginning to emerge from its darkest hour, but there was still much to do. I had heard a recording of Archie Norman speaking about the recovery of Asda at a conference, and felt this was a CEO and a business which wanted to really change things and go places. I felt that I wanted to be part of that vision. There was a real sense of urgency, purpose and excitement in the business, or so it seemed to me as I listened to the story. So it proved when I actually joined – the vibrancy was there, and this carried forward. Asda was number four of the big four supermarket retailers at that time. When I joined the Asda business, the big battle was between Tesco and Sainsbury over the number one position. Sainsbury was Tesco's enemy, and it was intent on taking the number one grocer title from them, which ultimately they did. Safeway was in third place in volume terms, and Asda was a definite fourth. I remember the press at the time saying that there was only room for 3 big players in the sector, and they were still predicting the potential demise of Asda. I felt this was a challenge, and a battle worth joining.

I wasn't alone in my desire to join the cause of making Asda a great business at that time. In the same year, Justin King (who became chief executive of Sainsburys in later years) had joined Asda as business unit director of beers/wines & spirits; Tony de Nunzio joined as finance director of Asda's Allied Maples group from l'Oreal (Tony became chief executive of Asda); and Andy Bond (who also became chief executive) joined Asda to run events in the marketing function. Many of the people joining Asda at that time have gone on to perform executive roles in Asda, and indeed gone on to even greater heights in other major businesses. There was a 'cadre' of talent replacing the whole of the top 200 executives at Asda, both from outside the business, and mixed with promotion of the best talent from within. Many talented imports came from Mars and were known and recruited by Allan Leighton (Justin King, and later Paul Mason; Richard Baker and Angela Spindler). Others came from an 'eclectic mix' of business, myself from British coal; Andy Bond from engineering and Tony deNunzio from l'Oreal.

This pool of talent proved extremely powerful in the renewal of the Asda business. There was a real desire to compete and be the best. Asda quickly became a 'can do' business. Asda was getting back to the roots of its early days, innovative, fast acting, with a powerful new culture 'the Asda way of working' as the enabler of change.

Within a short space of time, Asda had recruited 5 chief executives's, three for Asda (Paul Mason; Tony deNunzio; Andy Bond) and two went on to become chief executives in other businesses (Justin King at J Sainsbury; Richard Baker to Boots.) This was truly a talent revolution and a cultural revolution, and the mix was powerful.

Another addition to the cultural mix was Archie Norman's desire to make colleagues owners with a 'stake' in the business. The colleague share ownership plan gave colleagues a 'share in the game'; making them interested in the share price and the business performance, which was a useful additive to the momentum being created. To keep this momentum going, there were continual cultural stimuli and new ideas. Archie's own office administered a 'tell Archie' suggestion scheme for colleagues throughout the business to send in ideas for improving the business. This ran at a regular and amazing 20,000 ideas per year. Colleagues were awarded badges of recognition, for giving service to customers which was 'above and beyond the call of duty'. These were much treasured and proudly worn.

One idea, taken from a US fact finding tour to Wal-Mart (long before Asda was thought of as a prospective acquisition) was the volume producing item scheme. The basic idea was that any individual Asda colleague could order stock into store, and sell large quantities, by promoting it locally themselves. There were some extraordinary volume uplifts which resulted, and those who won that month, got the use of a company Jaguar for a month.

Beside these ideas, which were basically about invigorating shopfloor colleagues to sell and serve, there were ideas impacting the Asda house environment. Everyone throughout the whole of Asda wore a name badge, so that everyone was on first name terms. People wore red hats in the open plan office if they were writing a paper, or concentrating on a complex piece of work and didn't want to be disturbed. The 'golden cone' parking award was given to people for parking in the ten spaces right outside the front door at Asda house for one week. These spaces had previously been for the exclusive use of the chairman/chief executive and the board. The only way to get those spaces in the 'new' Asda culture, was if individuals were nominated by a store for giving them great service.

These cultural 'totems' began to change the attitude of colleagues to Asda's recovery plan. They were reinforcements of what Asda was seeking to achieve. None of these things were sufficiently significant alone to save the business. It was Archie Norman's ability to orchestrate all these elements which created the necessary momentum. At the end of the second year of the recovery plan, customer numbers were up to 4.5 million (an increase of 20%); operating profit was up

15% year on year, and like for like sales growth was a record breaking 12%.

My joining Asda during this exciting phase was initially to manage and build a trade union relationship, which had been broken during the dark days of near bankruptcy. This had been due to the strike threat sponsored by the union's regions over the pay freeze. My brief broadened over time to driving colleague engagement and create a healthy high performance culture. Before long, the challenges came thick and fast, and I was heading up the retail people function as well.

I remember being genuinely stimulated by the challenge of rebuilding a business and taking it back to greatness. It was hard graft, but enormously rewarding. Much worthwhile change is often exhausting….. it is certainly never easy. There were still a lot of management attitudes and behaviours to change. My listening groups with hourly paid colleagues in the business were often acutely painful to hear. They had a lot of things to get 'off their chest'! They say that feedback is the 'breakfast of champions', and it felt as if there was an awful lot of 'breakfast' to digest! Some days, I went home thinking that we would never overcome the huge negativity that employees felt for the business, and the leadership which had driven it into difficulty.

Nevertheless, problems were being systematically fixed, and momentum was gathering. The business focus was back to the core retail proposition, and Lofthouse foods (the manufacturing operation from Asda's early years) was sold, along with Allied Maples. Allied was sold to

Carpetland, whilst Maples was sold to its own management team. Asda had never found success in the furniture or the carpet retail arena.

By 1995, the debt mountain had disappeared, and Asda was cash positive. The three year recovery programme had been successful and Asda had established itself as 'Britains best value fresh food & clothing superstore' once again. Customer numbers by 1995 had climbed to 5.2 million per week. The business was no longer burdened by £1 billion of debt, and the net cash position was £4.2 million positive. This was the acid test of the 'recovery', and it had been largely built by cultural renewal.

At the end of the recovery period in 1995, the top 200 people in the Asda business were invited to a conference at one of Asda's distribution centres in Lutterworth (no big fancy hotel/conference venue).... a low cost 'in house' solution using some disused office space. This conference was for the unveiling of the business strategy for the next three years. I well remember the anticipation of the event, as Archie Norman & Allan Leighton led a 'tour de force' joint presentation of the ideas that would move Asda into the next 3 year horizon. There was an energy and a 'buzz' to the top 200 team, the business was being well led once again, and success was beginning to become a norm. Confidence was returning to the business.

In 1991, the headlines had been – 'Asda fights to stave off disasda'; 'superstore shambles wipes £16 million off Asda'; 'Asda profits warning ruins rally in market';

'Asda got a clue?' Whereas 3 years later, the headlines were all about 'stormin Norman' and 'It Asda be a recovery'. Archie Norman and his team had saved Asda from disaster, and turned it into a real force in British retailing.

The new strategy was to become 'Britain's fastest changing retailer', back to that successful vein of innovation which had been a key feature in Asda's early success with Peter Asquith & Noel Stockdale. Asda acquired the George Davis partnership, with the aim to make George clothing Britain's number two clothing brand (after Marks & Spencer). Asda also began to 'campaign' seriously for value for the customer. Asda was 'back' to being the customer value champion. Asda drove the abolition of the net book agreement in publishing, and exposed the exploitive pricing of medicines and vitamins, together with campaigns for the abolition of VAT on essentials such as feminine hygiene products. Asda was once again becoming a 'force for good' in the UK economy, exposing elements of 'rip off Britain' and acting as a real consumer advocate.

The business began to turn its thoughts to potential areas for growth at this time. There was a brief period of discussion about a merger with Safeway. There was no real optimism around whether the regulatory authorities would approve of such an action, but it was clear that the Asda business should look for a growth vehicle of some kind. Archie became chairman of Asda, and Allan Leighton was promoted to the position of chief executive. Archie had ambitions to go into public service as member of Parliament for Tunbridge Wells, but both were looking for a solution to the further growth of Asda.

First on the horizon was a potential merger with Kingfisher, which was hailed by the pundits as a synergistic opportunity for two retail giants to form a pan European food/general merchandise and clothing conglomerate. This began to flounder, based on disagreements about the personalities from the two company boards around who would get which top jobs on the new board. This heralded the discussions with Wal-Mart. The story of the Wal-Mart acquisition is contained in Appendix IV.

The end of Asda's history in the 1990's closed in a much different place to the previous decade. Asda was operating in a very different and growing culture. Asda had begun to develop a style which sought to get people on board and involved in the vision. People in the Asda business really felt they were working with a cause – providing great value and legendary service for customers. The road had not been smooth, and there were mistakes along the way, (this happens in all businesses) but Asda ended the 1990's with sales of over £6 billion; 6 million customers shopping every week and a share price of £1.20 (a far cry from 27p on the dark day when Archie Norman had arrived).

The developing culture at Asda was one which expected all colleagues to constantly look for innovation and radical solutions to make the business better. This was true of the ideas from 'tell Archie' (which sunsequently became 'tell Allan'), and also the cross functional positive action groups. It was accepted that people did new things and made mistakes. People felt empowered to do things, to challenge the 'status quo'. There was a very real sense in store listening groups that colleagues had learned they could tell you absolutely what they really did think. They had no fear of reprisal or recrimination. That kind of candour in an organisation is immensely powerful. As Allan Leighton remarks today, "Asda is the most powerful organisational culture of any I have ever seen."

Appendix 4

Asda enters the 21st century - acquisition into the Wal-Mart family 1999

> "The business of America is business"
>
> John Calvin Coolidge
>
> "That strange blend of the commercial traveller, the missionary and the barbarian conqueror, which was the American abroad"
>
> Olaf Stapledon
>
> "Our society distributes itself into barbarians, philistines and populace; whilst America is just ourselves, with the barbarians quite left out, and the populace nearly"
>
> George Arnold

I was representing Asda at an event to say 'thank you' to businesses who had released territorial soldiers for service in Iraq. Prince Charles asked me what it had been like to become part of Wal-Mart. His question was the question on the lips of most people I meet in business circles.

Working within the Wal-Mart family

The most commonly asked question from every candidate I have interviewed, since Wal-Mart acquired

Asda, has been "what's it like working with Wal-Mart?" Some people are in awe of the world's largest company, but many want to know the opportunities it presents and most are just fascinated. The same question is asked by consultants, and people Asda does business with, with the same range of expectations. I am assuming that, as a reader of a book about Asda, you will have exactly the same question yourself. So I will seek to answer it for you.

Aficionados of retail history will remember that Asda was about to merge with Kingfisher in 1999. The theory was that this would create a combined force in food and non food retailing which would be one of the largest in Europe, and would produce buying synergies and efficiencies which would make the newly formed entity a success. The problem was the usual merger discussion 'fall outs' over who was to get the top jobs. Sir Geoff Mulcahey wanted the lion's share of board seats for his own team, and Allan Leighton was less than happy with the potential outcomes for his own top team.

As a result, an approach was made to Wal-Mart (who had been interested in the UK market for some time), and the sale was completed in the week. You can read Allan's observations on the circumstances of the sale in his book 'On Leadership'. It's a fascinating personal insight into that time.

Who says large corporates cannot operate at speed. The then chief executive of Wal-Mart, David Glass, was a cautious businessman and wasn't sure about the deal. Asda was performing well in the market at the time, and consequently commanded a price premium. Acquisitions are more normally made when businesses are struggling, and the purchase price is low. However, the upcoming executive at Wal-Mart was Lee Scott, who subsequently became the next chief executive, was very keen to do the deal, and Asda was purchased by Wal-Mart in 1999 for £6.7billion.

Although Asda and Kingfisher were of a similar size, the merger had felt like an attempted takeover, and a clash of cultures. Whereas the purchase by Wal-Mart felt more like a merger on equal terms, despite being a clear purchase by a much larger business. Don Soderquist led the team who came to the UK to 'meet and greet' after the deal had been done, and he was a great ambassador for the Wal-Mart business. The word went out within Wal-Mart that Asda wasn't broken, and that people in the US shouldn't seek to fix it. Asda was the tenth business which Wal-Mart had purchased, and they had obviously learnt a lot in the buying of other businesses. They had learnt about systems conversion, about buying synergies, and about letting country management teams, in whom they had confidence, get on with the job.

The conversion to Wal-Mart systems in 1999/2000, which was named 'breakthrough', went extremely well. Asda was given a real piece of retail competitive edge at that time, without the need for a business case or any capital investment. To be handed 'state of the art' retail systems with reliability, without the need for major investment, was a huge business competitive advantage.

The other major advantage of the acquisition was the ability to purchase general merchandise products from around the world, using Wal-Mart's scale and access to markets. Asda was able to co-source at amazing prices, based on global volumes, and pass those savings onto customers. The acquisition also created a price expectation from Asda customers, together with potential new customers who had shopped at Wal-Mart in the US (especially near Disney in Florida). This resulted in an early sales boost arising from the acquisition.

It wasn't all about things Wal-Mart gave Asda. Asda was recognised by Wal-Mart for the expertise of its George clothing brand. Over the subsequent years, Wal-Mart sold George clothing in other markets around the world, and it is entirely conceivable that George will become the world's largest clothing brand through Wal-Mart's scale.

The other element which was very pleasing to me, is that Wal-Mart recognised Asda's expertise in people management. Many of Asda's national and European awards as 'best employer' occurred during the Wal-Mart ownership. Wal-Mart recognised that Asda had expertise they could make use of, both in the way the business communicated with colleagues (especially around pay/benefits/and recognition) and also in training and development innovation. One of Asda's people development concept was 'stores of learning'. These were stores designated as centres of best practice operation, used to train newly hired or promoted managers. This concept became a Wal-Mart global best practice, shared and used in all markets.

I personally received the Sam Walton award of international excellence, and I am very proud of that fact. However, I feel I received it on behalf of a very innovative people team and a very 'leading edge' people business at Asda. There are few American corporates who take learning from subsidiary business, but Wal-Mart is one such. It is part of their strength, and shows a maturity in acquisition which is atypical.

Wal-Mart instigated a performance bonus for all hourly paid colleagues, at a cost of approximately £20 million. This was something Asda may have wanted to do as a public limited company, but would have found it very difficult to do. City expectations would not have countenanced a £20 million dip in profits in one particular year. Wal-Mart instigated a performance bonus for all Asda colleagues as part of the acquisition. This was a huge fillip to the front line colleagues of Asda, and was a gift from Wal-Mart as a parent company. Interestingly, Wal-Mart gained no press coverage for that significant decision.

In summary, was the Wal-Mart acquisition a success? Yes it was. 80% of acquisitions fail and 20% succeed. The acquisition of Asda by Wal-Mart lies in that 20% range. Allan Leighton's view was that this was the best possible option for the future of Asda. Asda had for many years admired Wal-Mart's capabilities, and had copied a number of their retail ideas, long before the acquisition. Wal-Mart also thought the Asda business was more like Sam Walton's original stores than parts of Wal-Mart.

Allan reflects back on his time at Asda with some interesting thoughts. "Asda is not about culture, as some people understand it. There is something different about it. Asda is a 'cocktail' of things working together. The culture worked in turnaround and 'breakout', and it is still working. The culture has survived changes of leadership... it is so different... you can't see it, because it is all those small elements together" In fact, Allan Leighton lays down an interesting challenge. "Read this book because you wont be able to do it yourself".

Allan himself left Asda in 2000 to 'go plural', and has subsequently been involved with a plethora of businesses, perhaps most notably the Royal Mail where he was chairman for seven years. Allan was succeeded as chief executive at Asda by Paul Mason. Paul completed the conversion of Asda systems to the Wal-Mart Retail Platform by 2001, before himself becoming chief executive of Matalan, and being succeeded at Asda by Tony de Nunzio.

This is far from the end of the Asda story, since the pace of change continues, and the competitive nature of retailing drives continuous change. In 2005, Asda celebrated 40 years in retailing, facing new competitive challenges, and these were taken up with Andy Bond as chief executive. Tony de Nunzio CBE became chairman of Vendex in the Benelux countries. Asda faced a major strategic challenge, by not being allowed to acquire the Safeway business when it came to the market. The government of the day was determined to keep four distinct major players in the grocery sector, and Morrisons were the only viable bidder not restricted by that competition ruling. Asda had to utilise other growth vehicles in both format and dot com. But the Asda business continued to both grow and thrive.

Asda has a 'magic' to it, much of which is tied up in the culture. There is an intense pride amongst the people of Asda; a will to succeed, and a quirky sense of innovation and 'swimming upstream' against the accepted normal run of events.

As a reader, you may have been part of Asda's history. I hope I have captured the main elements for you, and I am sure some will remember other landmarks along the evolution of the Asda business. For those readers who have never been part of the Asda business, I trust my description was sufficiently informative to give you a clear picture of events.

Asda was an exciting business to be a part of, and certainly my fifteen years as part of the Asda story were some of the most exciting and rewarding of my career. I have not taken the story up to the present day, because of commercial sensitivity... maybe that will be the subject of a different book written by a different author in the future?

The Asda alumni

"Wisdom is knowing when to speak your mind and when to mind your speech."

Evangel

"A man doesn't begin to attain wisdom until he recognises he is no longer indispensible."

Richard E. Byrd

"Knowledge comes, but wisdom lingers. It may not be difficult to store up in the mind a vast quantity of facts within a comparatively short time, but the ability to form judgements requires the severe discipline of hard work and the tempering heat of experience and maturity."

Calvin Coolidge

"Wisdom is like electricity. There is no permanently wise man, but men capable of wisdom, who, being put into certain company, or other favourable conditions, become wise for a while, as glasses being rubbed acquire electric power for a while."

Ralph Waldo Emerson

Scattered throughout this book, you will have found commentary on the seven principles of building a high performance culture, from those I have termed the Asda alumni. They were all key 'players' in the business during my time at Asda, many of them actually running the business as chief executive. All of them went on to do some other interesting things.

I think it adds value to get their 'outside-in' perspective on the performance culture of Asda. I find that you can look back on things, with a very dispassionate and objective view, when you have moved on to doing something different.

There is a lot of ex Asda talent running a lot of UK and global retail businesses. This is not a surprise from my perspective. The Asda environment grew such a cadre of talent over the turnaround years, that it was almost inevitable that some proportion would 'escape' to do other things in different businesses.

Many newspapers have speculated as to why people have left Asda over the years, especially since Asda was such an engaging organisation. It appeared to be an enigma, but for me it was very simple. Many of the reasons for leaving were about individual life plans. They have varied by individual executive, but many wanted to run their own business. The 'draw' of being a FTSE top 100 chief executive, is compelling as a career path for 'top flight' executives, and Asda had a clutch of these growing up in the business. I think a mature talent strategy accepts that it is natural to let a few of your people 'fly' elsewhere. That opens new opportunities for growth within, and is a healthy atmosphere. If the top job is static for too long, the whole business waits for dead men's/women's shoes. Conversely, if you change too often, you can lose direction and continuity. It's a fine balance.

For me, the impressive thing about Asda, was that for every change of chief executive I was involved with, Asda had a strong internal candidate ready to take the helm. When Archie Norman became chairman, prior to becoming a conservative MP, Allan Leighton was ready to become chief executive. When Allan was involved with the deal to sell Asda to Wal-Mart, rather than follow through on the proposed merger with Kingfisher in 1999, Paul Mason was ready to become chief executive. Allan, of course went 'plural' and became chairman or non-executive director of so many businesses, the list seemed endless and included lastminute.com; Leeds united; Bhs; BSkyB; Selfridges and Loblaws in Canada.

When Paul Mason went to become chief executive of the clothing chain Matalan, the choice of chief executive was between Richard Baker and Tony de Nunzio. Tony became chief executive of Asda, with Richard as his chief operating officer for a while. It was inevitable that Richard (who wanted to become the chief executive of a FTSE plc by 40 years of age), would go and fulfil his potential. Richard Baker, as many business readers will know, became the chief executive of Boots, for the 5 years prior to leading the business into merger. When Tony de Nunzio left to become chairman of retail conglomerate Maxeda (in the Benelux countries), Andy Bond had already been groomed as the chief operating officer and was ready to become chief executive.

Because Asda grew this cadre of talent, the DNA of the business was never lost. Those becoming chief executive grew and developed with the business, and fully understood the culture. They were hired for their attitude and they 'got it', in terms of what made the business 'tick', and how to build a high performance culture. I believe it's pretty hard to become a chief executive from outside a business, and learn a new culture. That's why 80% of external appointments to chief executive fail. The Asda approach was to grow its own leaders.

It is not only Asda's chief executives and chief operating officers who have gone on to greatness. Justin King left Asda for the Marks & Spencer food business, and then went on to become chief executive at J Sainsbury. Justin appointed quite a sizeable team of ex Asda executives around him there. Ian McLeod left Asda to become trading director for Wal-Mart's problematic German operation, before running Celtic football club, and then becoming chief executive at Halfords. Ian then became chief executive of Coles, one of the largest retailers in Australia. Chris Pilling was Asda's marketing director, and became chief executive of First Direct, the online banking business.

I could go on, but I think I have made my point about the strength and depth of talent in the Asda business. If you hire great people, they will contribute massively to your business success. They will become a part of the 'magic'. My advice is not to worry if a few escape to take up the number one job elsewhere. There is only one chief executive role, and top talent can't be expected to wait forever.

One member of the Asda alumni comes from a slightly different angle. He has an outside-in perspective on Asda, but he still works for Wal-Mart. Dave Cheesewright was originally recruited to Asda in 1999, and so joined Wal-Mart from Mars. He became Asda's chief operating officer and chief merchandising officer, before taking up the position of chief executive of Wal-Mart's Canadian operation. His is an interesting perspective in that he worked in a different country, and now oversees Asda as part of a wider Wal-Mart portfolio.

I trust you will find it interesting to relate the commentary from the Asda Alumni on the seven principles of building a high performance culture. Having interviewed them all in the preparation for this book, I found it fascinating that they all had a 'special place in their heart' for the Asda business. There is something about the 'magic' of Asda which is more than a job. Also, you will have noted that they have all taken learnings from Asda and applied them to other business contexts. Good ideas work with people everywhere.

Lightning Source UK Ltd.
Milton Keynes UK
UKOW05f1955260913

218041UK00001B/3/P